BEETLE

OWNER'S SURVIVAL MANUAL

BEETLE
OWNER'S
SURVIVAL
MANUAL

JIM TYLER

ACKNOWLEDGEMENTS

First and foremost: Em, Dave and Chalkie for an education in car maintenance, repair and restoration. My pals at the Beetle Specialist Workshop for again allowing me the run of their restoration workshop.

Friends and family for their encouragement. Neighbours for their tolerance, good humour and occasional (unsolicited) pearls of wisdom. Osprey for publishing the book. Canon, Yashica and Zenith for making cameras tough enough to withstand life in my workshop and at BSW. And that's about it.

First published in Great Britain in 1995 by Osprey Publishing,
Elms Court, Chapel Way, Botley, Oxford OX2 9LP
E-mail: info@ospreypublishing.com

This edition published 2000

© Jim Tyler 1995

ISBN 1 85532 972 7

Editor • Shaun Barrington
Art Editor • Mike Moule
Designer • Leigh Jones

Printed and bound in Great Britain by The Bath Press

Contents

Introduction	6
Beetle – The Ultimate Survivor	**8**
Surviving Beetle purchase	12
Crime	17
Which Beetle?	20
Restoration project/usable Beetles	20
Custom Beetles	21
Restored Beetles	22
Survival for (and in) your Beetle	**26**
Safety	27
Weekly checks	29
Monthly Service	35
6 month Service	39
Annual Service	51
18 months /3 years	53
MOT	53
Look after your body	57
Creature comforts	59
Lights	66
In car entertainment	67
False economies	69

Surviving Restorers and Restoration	**71**
Surviving DIY restoration	73
Tools/facilities	76
Reconstruction vs restoration	77
Stripdown	89
Welded repairs	83
Paint preparation	88
Spraying equipment	92
Putting it back together	100
Surviving professional restoration	106
Pro-Am restorations	115
Surviving Breakdowns	**116**
Carburettors	116
Fuel injection	119
Electrics	120
Common faults	124
Flat tyre	130
Engine won't play ball	125
'Problem' cars	131
On-road breakdowns	134
Check list	138
Forecourt and service data	141
Index	**142**

Introduction

A friend of mine recently confessed to having – many years ago – bought 50 litres of best quality (VW branded) antifreeze for his recently acquired first Beetle 'from a man in a pub' – his excuse being that the antifreeze 'came at the right price' and was a good long-term investment; exactly how many pints of beer he had downed before making this investment is not known.

There is something of a dilemma here for the writer of a book dealing with the ownership and maintenance of a car in knowing exactly where to start, what you can safely assume the reader already knows about the car – do you begin by stating that it is not necessary to buy antifreeze, that you should not worry about not being able to find the choke control (because it's automatic), that you should not panic when you raise the 'bonnet' (hood) and discover that someone's stolen the engine, because Volkswagen has thoughtfully

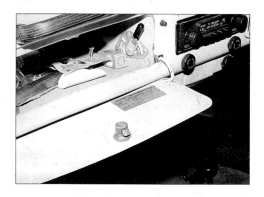

Absolute beginner's corner. The lever in the glove compartment unlocks the luggage bay lid and, if you're lucky, the sticker to the right of the lid gives the tyre pressures. NEVER over-inflate the front tyres, the car becomes almost uncontrollable!

provided a spare engine in the back? No. The author has to take a certain amount for granted.

If you happen to be an absolute novice Beetle owner and, having just collected your first Beetle, find yourself struggling to open the luggage compartment lid, operate the de-mister (such as it is) or open the fuel filler cover flap, just stop outside the first house you pass which has a Beetle parked in the driveway and knock on the door. Explain that you have just bought the Beetle, and ask how to do whatever it is confuses you. In my experience, any Beetle owner would be only too delighted to help, because Beetle owners are the friendliest of all car owners.

As the title of this book suggests, it is more concerned with the survival of the Beetle owner than with that of the car itself, though the two are inextricably linked. The motoring bookshelves are weighed down with practical books which describe in pictures and words how to do this or that – few bother to tell the reader what can go wrong, how to deal with things that go wrong – in other words, how, in The Real World (in a draughty and damp single garage with a typically inadequate set of tools, rather than in a photographic studio or a professional workshop), to *survive* doing whatever it is they describe.

But there's more to surviving Beetle ownership than spannering, and this book attempts to cover all of those areas which have the potential to jeopardise an otherwise untroubled relationship 'twixt owner and car. Here's a quick tour of the book.

History – Buying: The VW Beetle has a fascinating pre-production history and, with in excess of 80,000 recorded production modifications, one of the most complicated production histories of all cars. I have distilled some of the wealth of available information into the opening chapter, and concentrated on the major production milestones of this, the ultimate auto survivor.

Buying a Beetle is easy because there are always thousands in the market place to choose from, but there are pitfalls. Some of the cars are offered for sale illegally and, if you buy a stolen car on false plates or a car which is subject to outstanding loan repayments, you could lose both the car and your money. All European-manufactured Beetles are now old cars, and buying a Beetle which is not suffering extensive (usually hidden) bodyrot, which has been well maintained and which is not prone to frequent mechanical failure is anything *but* easy. Buying a Beetle is easy – surviving the experience is another matter altogether.

Maintenance: The Beetle is quite rightly regarded as one of the most rugged, most reliable and most easily maintained and repaired cars ever made. But the last European production Beetle left the factory back in 1977 – at the time of writing, seventeen years ago, and hence all UK Beetles saving the few personal imports from South America and Mexico are very old cars.

Like old people, elderly Beetles need a lot more attention than youngsters, and they need this Tender Loving Care on a more frequent basis if they are to give of their best. Neglect your Beetle and not only will it become less reliable, perhaps slower and possibly less well-behaved on the road, but long-term and potentially terminal problems will develop to the point at which you might have no alternative other than to spend a small fortune to make the car roadworthy, or even to take the car off the road for good. This book shows you how to care for your Beetle, but it is not a workshop manual, and it should be used in conjunction with a manual which relates to the specific year and model of your own car. This book covers basic maintenance procedures which, if adhered to, will enable your Beetle to survive and give you many years' happy motoring. (For those who wish to take on more, the publishers recommend *VW Beetle Preparation, Restoration, Maintenance* by, erm, Jim Tyler.)

Restoration: Many people don't survive classic car restoration; few first-time amateur restorers appreciate just how much work a full restoration entails (1,000 – 2,000 hours is not uncommon), just how many things can go seriously wrong or how much money it is possible to lavish on even so simple a car as the Beetle during a DIY restoration. Many have their Beetles restored by professionals and, although many such restorations progress smoothly, there are others which end in some degree of disagreement or occasionally serious dispute between the customer and the restorer. Whether you do it yourself or pay professionals to restore your pride and joy, this book describes how to survive Beetle restoration.

Breakdowns: The reliability of the Beetle is one of its most endearing features, but Beetles can and do break down. Whether the engine dies on the open road or refuses to fire up on the driveway at home, there is nothing so comforting as knowing that you possess the ability to identify and cure the fault. There are plenty of publications containing fault-finding guides but, as the number of possible causes for a non-starting engine is approximately 1,001, no such guide can be anywhere near comprehensive. I've approached fault-finding from another angle, by describing how components of the ignition and fuel systems operate and – armed with this information – you should be able to identify most of those 1,001 faults for yourself!

Happy Beetling!

Jim Tyler

CHAPTER ONE

Beetle – the Ultimate Survivor

What follows is no more than the briefest of histories; the Beetle has the longest production history of any car and has been subjected to over 80,000 factory modifications, and to cover any individual aspect of the pre-history or production history in any sort of detail would require a large book (or a small library) of its own.

It is a wonder that the Beetle survived to become a production car at all, let alone that it would become the best-selling car of all time. The car was conceived and born during a period of political and economic turmoil in Germany. Having gained absolute political authority, Chancellor Adolf Hitler was in a position to pursue his many visions, one of which was that, one day, every German worker would have his own personal motor transport and a network of roads fit to drive the cars on. The latter ambition saw the creation of the first autobahns; to realise the former, he turned to Dr. Ferdinand Porsche.

For many years it was accepted that Porsche and Porsche alone designed the Type 60 – the prototype Beetle – but more recently available information discredits this straightforward account. It appears that much of the credit for the design is in fact due to Tatra, the Czechoslovakian manufacturer. However, Porsche it certainly was who at the very least refined the design to the point at which prototypes could be produced.

To build Dr. Porsche's new car, a great factory complex, complete with workers' housing was constructed – 'Strength Through Joy' town – but before the Beetle entered mainstream production the second World War intervened.

The outbreak of World War Two was long believed to have put an end to Beetle production, but more recent evidence suggests that up to 1,500 Beetles were produced during the war years, the information having perhaps been suppressed because those cars – along with several military vehicles based on the Beetle – were built with what amounted to slave labour. There could have been little if any joy in 'Strength Through Joy' town during those dark days and, to make matters worse, in the closing stages of the war the Allied bombers rained destruction down on the factory.

Following the cessation of hostilities, the occupying forces were quite desperate for cheap motorised transport, and Officers from the British Army Royal Electrical and Mechanical Engineers (REME) were dispatched to the factory to see what could be salvaged and to assess whether car production could be re-established. A single complete Beetle remained in the bombed-out ruins of the factory. This was painted in matt green, shown to the military authorities, and an initial order for 20,000 cars was placed.

Any European motor manufacturer would have given his right arm for a 20,000 car order in the chaotic immediate post-war period, when raw materials were in short supply and the few potential customers with sufficient folding money to buy a new car could not be sold one unless their trade or calling – doctors, farmers etc. – made it an essential. Volkswagen – and their Beetle – had a flying start in life.

By 1950, Beetle production passed the 100,000 milestone. Five years on, the one millionth Beetle was produced. At a time when the mighty British motor industry was trying to

The Beetle is considered by many classic car enthusiasts to be somehow not a 'real' classic, so it's nice to see the occasional Beetle in a classic museum, like this one in Pembrokeshire, England.

pull itself up by its bootstraps, yet was still engaged in inter-company in-fighting, Volkswagen soared ahead.

In the UK, the motor industry was preoccupied with the essential business of manufacturing cars for export markets; foreign currency (particularly the US dollar) was needed if the very economy of the UK was to survive the immediate post-war years. Few UK industry chiefs could have lost sleep worrying about the competition posed by the quirky rear-engined Beetle but, when the Beetle production started to take off and quickly surpass that of all UK-built cars, even the UK motor industry mandarins began to sit up and take notice.

The immediate response to the growing success of the Beetle was (predictably) moves to try to prevent the cars from entering the UK domestic market and, in fact, it was not until the mid to late 1950s that the Beetle became a serious option for the UK car buyer. But the UK was (and still is) small fry as far as Volkswagen were concerned; the prize they wanted was the same as the UK manufacturers – a chunk of the massive US market. None was initially especially successful.

In a country where in the automotive sense bigger was accepted as better, neither the typical British saloon nor the Beetle was a natural seller. True, there were isolated success stories – the MGA sold over 80,000 in the States against less than 6,000 in its country of origin – but by and large, the North American market would only succumb to the Beetle's simple charms following the most amazing marketing program ever known in the motor trade – through which the Beetle Won the West.

Cars in the States sold on luxury, on their apparent level of refinement and mod cons, and on their sheer bulk – fuel being so cheap that no-one worried much about mpg figures. The Beetle was aggressively marketed as the antithesis of everything modern American consumerism stood for. It was cheap to buy and run, made few concessions to comfort and had

all the technical sophistication of a lawnmower – and this marketing worked. It took time, of course, to happen, but the breakthrough appears to have been the general acceptance of the car by young America. Dad still drove something the size of the average Thames barge, but the kids – they had the Beetle, and loved it.

The UK, too, was initially slow to take to the Beetle but steadily the little car gained its share of followers. Like many cars, the Beetle was most common in areas which contained one of the few major Beetle dealers – in other areas it could be as rare as hen's teeth. Judging by period feature films set in London, the Beetle seems to have been fairly prolific from the 'off' in the UK capital, because in many London 'street scenes' in the films of the '50s you'll see Beetles in the background. The home-grown Morris Minor almost single-handedly 'held the fort' for the domestic motor industry and prevented the intruder from swamping the market until sales of the 1959 Mini began to take off in the early 1960s. Today, all three cars are deservedly cult cars and recognised classics.

But sell the Beetle did. And those who bought it – loved it. It was almost certainly Beetle owners who were the first in the UK to form, if you like – an 'unofficial owners' club' – to adopt the practice of flashing headlamps and/or waving to other Beetle owners on the roads. Camaraderie was the name of the game and, even over three decades later on today's roads, the practice of greeting other Beetle drivers continues with, if anything, even greater enthusiasm.

MODELS

The earliest Beetles to find their way to the UK were split screens, but since the arrival of the oval more or less coincided with the start of official UK imports in mid 1953, splits are now very rare here. The first Beetles to be found in any quantity in the UK were the 1100, Standard or De Luxe (Export), the latter having

MacPherson strut. The major Beetle redesign came with the 1970 launch of the 1302/3. At the front, you'll find MacPherson strut suspension and, more importantly, at the rear double-jointed drive shafts – these combined to give a huge improvement in near-the-limit Beetle handling. Few people in Real Life, however, will ever drive anywhere near the limit, so don't feel that you have to pussy-foot around in a swing axle car.

hydraulic brakes and the luxury of a gearbox with synchromesh.

The 1200 Standard and De Luxe of 1954 had an extra 61 cc to boost power to 30 BHP and, perhaps equally as welcome, vacuum advanced ignition timing for better acceleration. The Standard had cable brakes, the De Luxe hydraulics. The De Luxe had, by 1961, a full synchromesh gearbox, 34 BHP, an anti-roll bar, the now-familiar automatic choke and a larger brake master cylinder.

The Karmann convertible came to the UK from 1954, three years after the first open top was made, but although over a quarter of a million of these convertibles were made, not too many came to the inclement UK. Hardly surprising when you consider that the UK exported the vast bulk of its own open-top sports cars.

The 1300 reached the UK in 1965, with a 40 BHP, 1285 cc engine. Six volt electrics persisted until 1968, but you did have the option of disc brakes at the front and dual circuit hydraulics. The 1500 – the last and most powerful of the swing-axle Beetles – arrived in 1966, although its 44 BHP was hardly a threat to the safety of the new motorways. Still, 80 mph was possible, and you did get dual circuit hydraulics and discs at the front.

Clearly *the* major re-design (1970) was the switch from torsion bars to MacPherson struts at the front and – more significantly – from swing axles to double joint drive shafts at the rear, of the 1302/1303/1303S models. These most refined of Beetles tamed the infamous tail-jacking tendency of earlier cars (which, truth be told, few people would have driven fast or recklessly enough to experience), and gave the motorist a little extra power to play with. But all of this was too little, too late for the European market and, in 1977, Europe kissed good-bye to the Beetle. But the Beetle survived and still survives (and even thrives) to this day in South America.

It was in fact inevitable that, one day, Europe and the Beetle would part company. Whilst VW soldiered on with the increasingly anachronistic Beetle, the rest of the motor manufacturing world had moved on and replaced older models – the Beetle's contemporaries – with much-improved alternatives. Volkswagen would have been acutely aware that they were being left behind and, from as far back as the early 1960s, VW had been trying to develop something more up-to-date. The 1963 Variant and the following variants of the Variant had been little more than a Beetle wearing more modern clothes – the air-cooled flat four still lived in the back – and it was not until 1970 that they had anything substantially different to offer.

VW took over NSU and, as a result, put the inherited K70 into production. Front-engined, front wheel drive and liquid cooled was as far from the Beetle as it was possible to get, but despite a production in excess of 200,000 the K70 was never going to be a replacement for the best-selling Beetle. The 1973 Passat was followed by the Beetle's spiritual successor and Volkswagen's salvation – the 1974 Golf, which surpassed ten million sales in the following fifteen years and which continues in revised form to the present day.

An excitable British motoring press got hold of a story in 1993 that the Mexican-made Beetle was to be re-imported into Europe – alas, it proved to be without substance. In fact, given the ever-more stringent European vehicle regulations, the Beetle could certainly not be sold as a mainstream car on the continent of its birth without modifications to meet crash and emissions criteria, modifications so substantial that they would probably lose the character of the car entirely. This does not, however, prevent personal imports and, if you want a brand new Beetle, there are companies advertising in the Beetle press who can help you realise your dream, so that – nearly half a century after the first Beetles reached these shores – you can drive a brand-new example of the greatest survivor in the automotive world.

SURVIVING BEETLE PURCHASE

There are plenty of buyers' guides which tell you where to poke suspect bodywork, what to look and listen for when the car is underway – Beetle Restoration/Preparation/Maintenance (Osprey Automotive) contains a buyers' guide running to approximately 20,000 words. What follows is not a Beetle Buyers' Guide – it is a guide to surviving Beetle purchase – which is another matter altogether.

Ask yourself this; if you now owned a good-

Heater channel rot. Proper heater channel replacement is a bodyshell-off, very major repair – so the heater channels get bodged. If you find holes or welded-on cover patches on a car you're thinking of buying, then think again.

looking and reliable Beetle, which you knew to be structurally sound – would you sell it? No, and neither would anyone else. OK., suppose that you were forced by some circumstances beyond your control to sell your beautiful Beetle – would you let it go cheaply? No, and neither would anyone else. Face facts; you are unlikely to be able to buy a really good Beetle cheaply.

On the other hand, if you suddenly discovered that your Beetle had serious rot which would cost a fortune to put right, or looming mechanical repair bills, would you then want to sell it? Of course you would.

If you wish to buy a Beetle, it is as well to accept from the outset the fact that you are about to enter a minefield. There are an awful lot of Beetles on the market to choose from – more, probably, than any other classic car – but a sizeable proportion of the cars you go to view can turn out to possess extensive rot which will prove ultimately to be very expensive to rectify properly, and rot which is easily (and is often) camouflaged.

The Beetle is not alone in this respect; in fact, most classic cars of a similar value which come to the market do so because their owners realise just how much it is going to cost them to make their cars sound and, because the consequent value of the car will not be high enough to justify proper repair, they bodge the cars. They use – honestly – chicken wire, hardboard, cardboard, newspaper, cement, papier-mâché, plaster, baked bean tins and, of course, GRP, in conjunction with lashings of bodyfiller to make their rotting and unsafe cars appear sound and roadworthy – smart, even. They then pass the problems onto someone else when they sell the car and hope that the new owner doesn't discover their misdeeds too quickly.

Not all bodgers are amateurs; some back-street bodyshops are staffed by gifted bodgers who can transform a car using only a few pounds' worth of bodyfiller. The most skilled bodgers can turn a scrap car into a looker which can only be recognised for what it really is following close inspection by an expert in assessing the cars: many people don't look closely enough and can be fooled by the camouflage – most are bedazzled by the shiny new paintwork, wild wheels and other bolt-on goodies.

The Beetle's great strength as a long-term survivor is its simple rugged construction; the backbone provided by the massive spine chassis means that the bodywork generally – heater

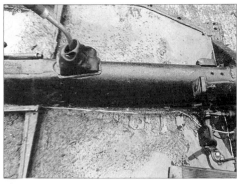

Chassis spine. The Beetle has a rugged spine chassis, and only the very worst examples (usually cars left idle out in the open for years or cars used extensively off-road and hence to be avoided at all-costs) will have any rot in the spine.

channels and the flitch panels on later cars excepted – can deteriorate to the stage at which a monocoque car would be hopelessly weakened to the point of being totally beyond economic repair, but the Beetle will still be essentially sound where it matters. Be warned, however, that spine chasses and frame heads *do* rot (frame heads can also be bent by frontal collision), so that, even though such rot is rare and irrespective of the state of the rest of the bodywork, you should always take the time to

Immediate chassis rejection. Lift the rubber mat and take a look at the sides of the spine just above floor level and – if you find rot – then you really ought to find another car.

Rot in the bumper mounting points is an MOT test fail point, but the area around the rear bumper mounts is often plastered with a thick layer of mud. Scrape it off to have a good look.

check whether you are looking at one of those rare cases with chassis rot.

However, the Beetle with substantial body-rot in panels which – on monocoques – are structural gets its annual certificate of roadworthiness (the MOT in the UK) provided that none of the rotting panels have sharp edges which could injure pedestrians (they're repaired with GRP, bodyfiller etc.); the Beetle stays on the road for another twelvemonth, the monocoque is towed away to the scrap yard. In time, the Beetle accrues so many of these cosmetic 'repairs' that making the car wholesome again really demands that entire body pressings are cut out and replaced. It is at this point that many Beetles are given their final 'tart-up' and offered for sale… Tread carefully in the Beetle minefield.

GETTING SOME 'EXPERT' HELP

Genning up on The Points To Look For won't do you any good if you are the type who lets your heart rule your head – in such cases, any faults which the car may have will simply be outside the periphery of your vision, or you may look at some glaring fault but fail to register its presence in your train of thought. You require a steadying influence – someone who knows about Beetles but who can appraise a car impartially because he is not buying the car for himself.

Finding a Beetle expert is easy – join the nearest branch of one of the National Beetle clubs. Every club has someone who knows enough not to buy a lemon (normally someone who has in the past bought one and who has learned from the experience) and many clubs

The restoration project car. The difference between a £200 MOT failure Beetle and one with an MOT and therefore costing ten times that amount can be that the latter has more welded-on cover patches. If you want a restoration project car then seek above all an 'honest' car – meaning one with honest bodyrot rather than a car which doesn't look too bad but which has been bodged.

A car which has been standing in long grass for any length of time can suffer severe rot in the lower wheel-arches, the floorpans, and even the frame head and chassis spine. Expect most fittings to be seized solid.

This was once a very sweet engine – a few years spent languishing in the corner of a field, however, has left it seized.

will have at least one member who has restored a Beetle and maybe one who has trained in the motor trade.

There are other sources of tame expert. Almost any garage mechanic will have experience of the Beetle and, even if they cannot tell you too much about the finer points of bodywork evaluation, they will most certainly be able to spot the real lemon and be more than competent at finding any mechanical problems.

If you're intending to spend a lot of money on a first-class Beetle, it is worth considering commissioning a motor engineer's report – not cheap, but these lads ought to be able to give you the most thorough appraisal possible and, if they prevent you from inadvertently spending a small fortune buying a tarted-up pile of junk, then the expense is easily justified.

If you're looking in the Bargain Basement, a motor engineer's report can cost nearly as much as the asking price of the car. A cheaper route to a professional opinion (albeit not so

15

Heavy frontal impact means that this Beetle is – sadly – best considered a source of spares. Cars with lighter damage might have their external panelwork straightened but could have a mis-aligned front suspension. Caveat emptor.

The torsion bar assembly is tough but poorly repaired crash damage can bend the tubes. A motor engineer or professional restorer ought to spot such problems and, if you're paying a high price for a really nice looking Beetle, it's worth forking out for a professional check-over.

comprehensive) is to submit the car for an MOT test – you can MOT test any car, any time – and it won't hurt to ask the tester to pay special attention to the state of the bodywork. If a vendor won't allow you to MOT test the car or have it examined by an auto engineer, it's because they are fully aware that the test will reveal problems sufficient to put you off buying the car. They are saving both you and themselves wasted effort and money.

WALK AWAY

Walking away from a Beetle is never easy; there are always those nagging doubts that maybe your conclusions on the condition of the car were too harsh, that maybe you're missing a real bargain. It's even worse if you reject a car on the grounds that tell-tale clues hinted of serious problems such as bodyrot or tired mechanical components, but you failed to find proof positive of such faults. Worse still is rejecting a car which seems OK but which isn't quite what you want – maybe the colour's not right, maybe it's not the version you'd set your heart on, maybe there's something not quite 'right' about the car or (equally important) the vendor. There is a way to prepare yourself mentally to be able to walk away from a car without that awful empty feeling which accompanies doubts that you might be turning down a bargain.

When you set out to view a car, convince yourself that it probably won't meet your standards, that you are not viewing it because you want to buy it – you're only going for a look. Think to yourself "I'm *not* going to buy this car, it will probably be a pile of junk, but it will be interesting to take a look at it".

When you view the car, think negative. Look for faults and be picky. Unless by some miracle the car *is* in good order and turns out to be exactly what you are looking for, keep concentrating on the minus points until you are genuinely convinced that this is not the car for you. Walk away.

Then it's time for some positive thinking. Don't brood over the possibility that you might have made a bad decision in rejecting, concentrate on the fact that something better will turn up. This is not a form of self-deception; something better *always* turns up!

CRIME

You know it already, but it must be emphasised: as a potential car buyer you face the hazard of inadvertently handing over money in

exchange for a car which the vendor is not, for a variety of reasons, at liberty to sell. Beetles are stolen, given false registration number plates and sold to unsuspecting buyers. Beetles which are in a person's temporary custody but which do not belong to them are sold. Beetles which are the subject of outstanding finance (loan repayments) and therefore the property of a finance company are sold. In each and every case, when the fraud comes to light, the poor buyer loses not only the car but usually his or her money.

Even worse, some prospective car buyers have set off to pay for and take collection of a car with large amounts of folding currency about their person, only to be robbed by the 'vendor'. Never, ever, set out with a lot of cash to buy a car.

A UK company called HPI Autodata (Tel. 01722 422422) keep listings of stolen cars, insurance write-offs, cars with outstanding finance and so on. For years, car dealers have been able to contact the company and, for a fee, have any vehicle they are thinking of buying checked out. The service is also open to the general public. HPI don't absolutely guarantee that a car is legitimate.

MORE SAFEGUARDS

Your first contact with a vendor is normally via the telephone when you reply to an advertisement. Firstly, to help guard against dealing with an undisclosed trader (the type who tart cars up for sale in their spare time) begin by saying that you are calling about 'the car' – not specifying which car. The part-time dealer will then ask which car you refer to, so put the phone down.

Insist on viewing the car at the vendor's home – never arrange to meet him or her anywhere else unless you relish the chance of getting mugged or sold a 'hot' car, and try to ensure that you are going to the vendor's own home, which should be the address given on the Vehicle Registration Document and which should house the advert's telephone number.

A restoration project car might not look very promising – what counts is what it's like underneath the skin.

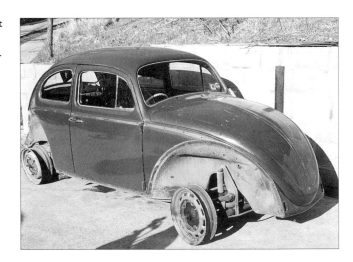

Surface rusting. This door can be – in fact it was – salvaged. Steel with surface rusting can be cleaned bright and re-painted. However, if you find rusting this high up on a car, you can bet your bottom dollar that there will be full-blown body-rot further down.

This car obviously needs new heater channels. Many cars with this sort of rust are, however, 'repaired' with non-ferrous materials (GRP and bodyfiller are the favourites). This is an 'honest' car – many are not, so beware.

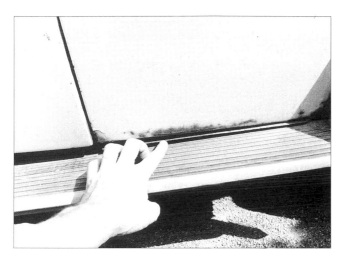

This is the base of the quarter panel. Surface rusting here usually indicates more advanced deterioration of the heater channel steel and the floorpan edge, so check carefully.

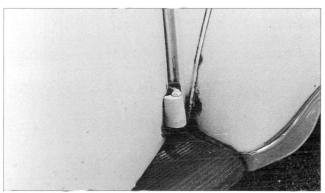

Surface rusting at the base of the A post usually accompanies rotting heater channels, and the rusting usually extends well across the base of the flitch panel.

Torsion bar Beetles feed all stresses from the suspension directly into chassis components, whereas the MacPherson strut models feed front wheel stresses into the flitch panel, shown here. I personally would never buy a Beetle which had welded patch repairs to the flitch panels around the strut mounting area.

WHICH BEETLE?

If you start out by defining exactly what you are looking for in a Beetle, you can save a lot of what would otherwise be wasted time in going to view cars which don't meet your basic criteria.

RESTORATION PROJECT BEETLES

Never make the mistake of paying too much for a restoration project car, and remember that the only difference between a £200 MOT failure car and one priced at five times that amount can be that the latter possesses more bodged repairs and a suspect MOT certificate.

That said, it is worth stumping up more to buy a car which has been well maintained and looked after, which is therefore mechanically sound, which has a good interior and good exterior trim, but which has failed the MOT test on bodywork problems. People tend to be intimidated by bodywork restoration whereas, in reality, it should be the costs of making a generally poor car mechanically sound and of replacing tired trim, electrics, hydraulics and so on which frightens them. It would be a poor Beetle which required more than twenty or so repair or replacement body panels, but just stop and consider how many mechanical, electrical, hydraulic and trim components – plus their fittings – there are in even so simple a car as the Beetle – there are thousands. Replacing that little lot will cost a lot more than a few repair panels.

The very best restoration project car is one which has been regularly maintained and used on the road right up to the day that the MOT failure certificate (for bodyrot) was issued. Because the owners erroneously believe that bodywork restoration costs are horrendous, they dump real restoration project gems. Advertisements for such cars usually state 'Welding needed for MOT'.

Look for the telltale signs of frequent servicing – a clean engine bay and fairly new ignition components, oil on the dipstick which doesn't resemble tar – that sort of thing. Check out the state of screw and bolt heads – butchered fastenings mean that the persons who worked on the car possessed only poor quality tools, and any unseen fastenings will of course be similarly damaged.

On the bodywork front, look for a car which has not been bodged. OK, that's a tall order, I know, but such cars *do* exist, and it is far easier to carry out bodywork restoration on a shell with honest and obvious rot than it is on one which some bodger has lavished his attentions.

USABLE BEETLES

If you're looking for a reliable Beetle and one which is not going to need expensive bodywork repair come MOT time, then the awful truth is that you're going to have to part with quite a lot of the folding stuff to realise your ambitions – the fact being, as we established at the start of this section, that no-one in their right mind lets a good Beetle go cheaply.

Because you're spending real money, the cost of commissioning a motor engineer's report – which will examine both mechanical and bodywork condition – becomes more acceptable.

At the very least, get an experienced mechanic to check out the car and – equally importantly – an experienced Beetle owner to test drive it. Someone who drives a Beetle every day will sense many potential problems with the engine, transmission and suspension which even a professional mechanic might not spot. OK, the test driver might not be able to tell you exactly what is wrong with the car, but at least they will be able to warn you that something isn't right.

Some of the Beetle trade specialists buy in, repair as necessary and sell Beetles – with some guarantees. These cars aren't cheap, but in theory at least they should be safe. Buy from a well-established dealer and you should not go far wrong.

CUSTOM BEETLES

Many 'custom' cars are in fact (under the skin) bodged cars – the Beetle is no better nor worse in this respect than any other car. Try not to look at the lustre of the paintwork – that will only cloud your judgement. It's what lies under that shiny paint which matters. The alarm bells should start ringing if a car you go to view has excessive applications of bodyfiller, often used to hide poor attempts at de-seaming (the seam

The immortal Beach Buggy. Some people have converted Beetles into Buggies because the Beetle's bodywork was rotten. This is fine as long as they make the chassis sound – many don't, and so there are a lot of questionable Buggies around. Don't be swayed by fat tyres and lots of chrome – if you cannot tell the peach from the lemon then you need expert help, not only to save money, but also, maybe, to stay safe .

is hammered inwards) and often used to fair-in rusted wings. Rust loves nothing better than being covered in bodyfiller; gives it a chance to spread underneath and mutate into full-blown rot. Take a magnet and use it.

The safest customs are those based on recognised kits – usually comprising bolt-on and/or glassed-on GRP panels. The important points to check are obviously the standard of workmanship which went into the customisation, the structural state of the car (many people blow their money on custom kits rather than boring old essentials like chassis repair) and – most importantly – the safety factor. The electrics, fuel and brake hydraulics must be in first-class condition – GRP cars can burn to a frazzle in minutes.

Some customs are essentially Beetles but with a lowered ride height and dressed up with

There are a number of off-road chassis to which Beetle engines have been bolted; there are also a lot of dubious DIY lash-ups – so take care. This Beetle rail is far more capable than the Mini-based example behind it, if only because it offers better ground clearance, plus the thrills of rear wheel drive.

a host of bolt-on goodies, the costs of which can be staggering and the combined effect of which can be stunning. The vendor is not going to recoup more than a fraction of the costs of the shiny bits, and don't be tempted to pay over the odds for what could turn out to be an over-dressed very average Beetle.

Good custom Beetles are usually well-known, and their customisers have well-justified reputations on the show circuit. These – along with professional companies which customise cars – are the safest people to buy from.

RESTORED BEETLES

Quality Beetle restoration – DIY as well as professional – is not exactly cheap, and quality restored Beetles rightly attract a premium price. However, a high asking price should not be regarded as an indication of quality workmanship, so unless you really know what you're doing, either bring in an expert (your nearest friendly Beetle restorer is as good a choice as any) or seek out a car professionally restored by a reputable company.

There is no excuse for a restorer – DIY or 'professional – not keeping a full photographic record of his work. A photographic restoration record becomes a part of the history of the subject car, adding to its aesthetic as well as its fiscal value and – importantly – providing future purchasers with proof positive that the restoration was carried out to a high standard.

No pictures – no sale – and make damn sure that the car in the photos is the one you're actually buying.

Even the most inexpert can weed out some poorly restored Beetles by paying attention to small details. Are screw and bolt heads, for instance, mis-shapen? If so, then poor quality tools were used by the restorer, and the state of screw and bolt heads is a good indicator that unseen components will be similarly butchered. Check out areas of bodywork where part repair panel welds lines are normally found – the quarter panel, A and B post lower sections and flitch. Look and feel (run your fingertips along

the panel) carefully for rivelling, for proud or swelling bodyfiller. Use a magnet to seek out really thick applications of bodyfiller or –

Even the most dyed-in-the-wool traditionalist must surely admire a custom beauty like this from Gary Berg. All that glisters, however, is not gold and, in some cases, it can take an expert to tell the difference between a bodged and a genuine show-standard custom Beetle. Some of the very worst bodges I've ever seen perpetrated on cars were the work of DIY 'customisers'. Price or the external looks of the car alone are no indicator of quality – find an expert to assess custom cars for you. (Photo: Mike Key)

Restoration at its best. The professionally restored Beetle will have cost its owner a lot of money – if you're offered an apparently superb Beetle at anything other than a high price, sniff the air and you'll smell a rat.

For the price of a completely anonymous and characterless bargain basement new small car of dubious build quality and possessed of searing depreciation, you could own a 'new, second-hand' Beetle.

This is the only way to deal with a rusty flitch top on a MacPherson strut car – cut the panel out and replace it – and it is one of the nastiest and most difficult of restoration jobs to carry out.

This is (with the exception of the rear lower edge) the only part of the flitch on a MacPherson strut car which should ever be repaired rather than replaced.

worse – holes bridged with GRP. These can appear almost anywhere on the car, but filler in the A post, B post or any area of the roof can reveal a car which has received a side impact or – in the case of filler in the roof – which has been rolled.

IN CONCLUSION:

Whether your life as a Beetle owner is a joy or a nightmare depends solely on whether or not you buy a good example. Buy a poor Beetle and you've fallen at the first fence. Bide your time until a good Beetle comes your way and enjoy years of trouble-free motoring.

If you're checking out a restored car, take a look under the rear seat base. You'll soon see whether the car has received a true bare-metal respray by checking the insides of repair panels.

CHAPTER TWO

Survival for (and in) your Beetle

The simple and robust mechanical components of the Beetle help ensure that individual examples can give huge mileages before serious mechanical attention is called for – in fact, most of the Beetles which are eventually towed away to the scrapyard are victims of bodyrot rather than terminal mechanical troubles. But all Beetles (save any personal imports from Mexico) are now old cars – the last European having left the production line back in the late 1970s and, like old people, they require lots of attention if they are to remain fit and healthy.

A well maintained Beetle which is driven hard will usually outlast a neglected one which is given only occasional and light usage. In fact, those who are in the habit of locking away their Beetles for months on end during the winter should be aware that cars tend to age more quickly if left idle for long periods than they do if given regular usage. If you are in the habit of laying your Beetle up for the winter, it is no bad thing to fire up the engine every couple of weeks and run it up to the normal operating temperature; the generator charges the battery at a goodly rate after a cold start and, in addition to keeping the battery in better order, by running the engine you are getting oil circulating around inside.

Maintenance in general comprises a set of routines which should be performed at differing intervals according to the length of time since last attended to or the miles travelled. The problem with trying to recommend hard and fast service intervals for any classic car is the fact that the recommendations should take into account not only the age and condition of the car, but also whether it has been driven hard in harsh conditions, or used lightly only on sunny Sunday outings.

There are two types of maintenance: on a weekly and a monthly basis, a number of checks need to be made to ensure that there are no developing problems which, if not rectified, can mature into serious and expensive faults. This work requires very little in the way of tools and facilities and is within the abilities of anyone. The frequency of this servicing

Maintenance toolkit. You don't need a huge toolkit to carry out basic maintenance – this is all that's necessary, and it should cost less than a 3-month service at a fairly upmarket garage.

would make Beetle ownership a very expensive exercise if you were to have it carried out professionally – sadly, most people ignore it altogether, and then wonder why their car occasionally lets them down! The second aspect of maintenance involves actually working on the car, and is necessary at three, six and twelve month intervals. The range of equipment needed grows in each instance – you need more tools for a twelve month service than for a six month service, and the skills and knowledge requirement similarly increases.

However, an entire maintenance toolkit can be purchased for less than the cost of having a single large (annual) service carried out professionally, and so any outlay on tools, equipment and consumables is quickly recouped.

Maintenance routines are presented here in 'menu' form, to enable those unsure of their own abilities to decide exactly what tasks they feel comfortable with, and which, if any, should be entrusted to professionals.

It is strongly recommended that you obtain a workshop manual which deals in detail with the specific model and year of your own Beetle – most especially for North American cars fitted with fuel injection. During its long production life, the Beetle has been subjected to tens of thousands of modifications, and not even the largest workshop manual could pretend to be truly comprehensive for all years and models of the Beetle. The kind of data which you will have to get from a workshop manual includes tightening torques, ignition timing settings and similar technical specifications.

SAFETY

Whenever you raise one end or side of the car, place chocks fore and aft of the wheels which will remain on terra firma. Only use a jack on firm, level, ground. On tarmac (especially in hot weather when the tarmac is soft) use a thick plywood board under the jack to spread the load. Preferably, use the jack and axle stands on a good concrete surface. Remember

Wheel chocks need not be anything special – bricks or breeze blocks, lumps of wood – anything is better than nothing (and nothing is plain stupid).

Beetle jacked up – front. The sturdy frame head is the obvious place to put your jack; use wood packing to protect the paint/underseal.

When raising or lowering the car, keep the jack at arm's length – just in case.

Safety first. Don't work underneath the car until it's been lowered onto axle stands.

Beetle jacked up – rear. Jack the rear of the car up by the back end of the spine – NOT the engine or transaxle casings, which can crack.

Beetle jacked up – side. The jacking points are under the heater channel. If these are starting to rot then you'll hear crunching noises as they crumple. Use these jacking points for roadside wheel changes.

that a jack is a lifting device – it is not intended to support weight – and so lower the raised car onto axle stands, and ensure that it is stable before carrying out any work underneath it.

Many people have a rather cavalier attitude to the car's electrics, because it is 'only' six volts or twelve volts, whereas the mains electricity (of which most are terrified) is two hundred and forty volts. The starter motor can draw as much power from the battery as would be needed to run two domestic mains electric heaters – think about that. Don't be fooled by the lower voltage of the car's electrical system; if you manage to short a circuit (see chapter four) then the battery discharges through it at a higher amperage than the wire can cope with; the insulation will melt, catch fire, and your precious Beetle could be on fire within a minute. Always disconnect the battery (earth strap first) before doing anything involving the electrical system.

Finally, many materials used in the car's construction, most brake fluids and, of course, petrol, are highly inflammable. When you are working on a car, the fire hazard is ever-present, so don't smoke or use a naked flame near anything combustible. North American cars: remember that fuel injection systems incorporate a device which maintains 25-35psi or greater pressure within the system, even when the engine is switched off – don't meddle with fuel injection!

WEEKLY CHECKS

It is no bad thing to adopt a regular routine for carrying out these checks – say, half an hour on Saturday mornings; most people seem to wash their cars once a week and supplementing the wash and valet with a few simple maintenance checks won't add much to the time required. The object is to carry out a number of checks which can highlight developing problems and allow them to be attended to before they deteriorate into expensive faults or result in on-road breakdowns. The only equipment required is a jack (a small trolley jack or bottle jack is preferable to other types, though the jack you carry in the car will suffice if necessary), a pair of axle stands, a foot pump for pumping up tyres, a tyre pressure gauge, a wire brush and some emery cloth. In addition, it pays to keep a small stock of servicing consumables – engine oil, hydraulic fluid for the brakes and distilled water for the battery.

Bottle or scissors jacks are OK for roadside wheel changes – do make sure they've got enough travel, though – this small scissors jack won't lift the tyres from the ground!

Checking the dipstick You don't have to fill the engine to the absolute maximum mark on the dipstick; the level should, however, be nearer 'Max' than to 'Min'.

ENGINE OIL

The Beetle's engine and gearbox are often described as 'unburstable', but a neglected or abused Beetle engine will last no longer than any other – in fact, in one important respect the flat four is more vulnerable to neglect than liquid-cooled alternatives.

Although the Beetle engine is commonly referred to as being 'air-cooled', it is for the most part cooled by a liquid – in this case, the engine oil. This passes through and is cooled in a radiator situated within the fan shroud. Neglect to maintain an adequate oil level and the engine will quickly overheat just like a liquid-cooled engine with an empty radiator – the difference being that the accompanying lack of lubrication in the flat four will more rapidly result in seizure and probable terminal damage to the engine.

Whereas the temperature control system for water-cooled engines is a thermostat which regulates the flow of coolant to the radiator, on the Beetle a thermostat mechanically operates flaps in the fan shroud – if the event of this failing to open the flaps, the oil radiator receives a constant flow of increasingly hot air and the engine overheats alarmingly in a very short space of time. The engine oil level and condition (and the oil strainer) and the ther-

Engine oil. Use a small pouring container of known capacity to fill your engine oil – it is very difficult to pour without spillage otherwise. This is a former 2-stroke oil container of 500ml – five fills of this gives 2.5 litres – the correct amount for the Beetle.

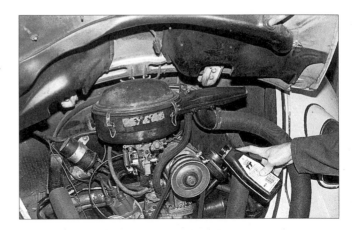

Move the air intake and breather pipes out of the way, offer up the bottle then tip it up into the filler neck in one smooth movement – no spillage!

mostat cannot be checked too regularly!

Lift the engine compartment lid and pull out the dipstick. Wipe the end of this and replace it, then withdraw it again and hold it horizontally. You will see two marks which indicate the maximum (top) and minimum acceptable oil levels. If the level is low, top it up – transferring the oil firstly into a small pouring bottle, it being very difficult to top up the Beetle using a five litre container. Pour in half a pint (500ml) or so, leave it a minute to drain down into the sump, then re-test the level.

Do not pour in too much in one go for fear of over-filling the engine – too much oil is nearly as bad as too little! The oil does not *have*

to come right up to the maximum dipstick mark – as long as it's somewhere over half way full as indicated by the two marks it will do for another week.

If you do inadvertently over-fill the engine, the excess will have to be drained out. I prefer to do this with the engine cold – scalding hot oil is not kind to your skin! Place a suitable receptacle under the drain plug on the bottom face of the crankcase, and carefully undo the plug – it is best to give it the last few turns by hand so that you can quickly replace it once a small quantity of oil has drained, so wear a disposable plastic glove throughout to keep the oil off your hands.

If the oil level is substantially down, then the engine is either losing or burning oil – the former will be apparent as an oil slick underneath the car after it has been parked overnight, the latter as blue smoke coming out of the exhaust tail pipes. In either case, remedial action is needed before the car is used on the road. A slow oil loss might quicken part-way through a journey and, as already stated, a Beetle run for any distance with low engine oil is doomed – overheating and internal friction leading to engine seizure being the most likely outcome. Oil which is burning in the combustion chambers can enter them either past (worn) piston rings or in between worn valve stems and guides, so that an engine or possibly a cylinder head overhaul will be needed. Either seek professional advice or take a deep breath and get yourself a good workshop manual!

GENERATOR DRIVE BELT

Still in the engine compartment, check the generator drive belt deflection. Under firm pressure from your thumb, the belt should deflect by no more than half an inch (12.5 mm) – if it proves slack, then it might not drive the generator and, more importantly, the cooling fan

Checking generator drive belt deflection. If the generator drive belt is too slack, the engine might not be cooled sufficiently because the fan isn't turning, plus the generator might not charge the battery – if the belt is too tight, you will eventually inevitably wreck the generator bearings.

properly, leading to battery drain and engine overheating respectively. Do not be tempted to over-tighten the belt, either, because this will place unacceptably high stresses on the generator bearings. Check the belt visually for wear and damage and replace if necessary. See under '6 month servicing' for details of tightening the generator drive belt.

Visually check the condition of wiring in the engine bay (there's not much), looking for damaged or discoloured insulation. If a previously clean wire now has a brownish discoloration, then it is for some reason taking too high a current, probably due to a short to earth somewhere within its circuit – disconnect the battery immediately and don't use the car until the problem has been rectified! Left unattended, the wire could eventually burn away its insulation and start an electric fire. If you want to learn more about electrics, read chapter four.

Check that the air ducting within the engine bay is all connected up correctly and that none is damaged. Check that none of the cheese-headed set screws which fasten the tin-ware are loose.

Under the car, visually check the brake back plates for leakage, which could turn out to be axle oil (at the rear of the car) or brake fluid. In either case, the leak should be traced and rectified before the car is used on the road. Any workshop manual should included step by step instructions for replacing the oil seal or wheel cylinder seals.

THERMOSTAT

The thermostat is hidden away underneath the engine and is protected by a steel pressing. To carry out a proper check of the thermostat it is necessary to remove the cover plate and measure the length of the thermostat, but in practice you can see enough of the 'stat (using a torch for illumination if necessary) to visually check that, with the engine warmed to normal operating temperature, the thermostat has

Checking thermostat. If the thermostat fails, the engine overheats. If the engine overheats, it can be terminally damaged. Dirty and not terribly pleasant though it may be, it's worth checking the thermostat frequently. A few misguided souls have been known to disconnect the linkage from the thermostat in the belief that this will make the engine run cooler – what happens is that the flaps in the fan shroud fail to open and the engine quickly overheats.

extended to just under 2" (46mm). An alternative to a visual check is to take a length of stiff wire, (12" of coathanger wire would be ideal) place a sharp 90 degree bend 2" from the end and trim to 1.8". You can offer this up to the thermostat and accurately check that it has extended sufficiently. While you are lying on your side on the ground, have a look around for oil leaks and check the exhaust and heat exchangers for signs of blowing (carbon deposits). A blowing exhaust requires immediate attention – either welded repair or replacement (temporary exhaust repair materials don't generally last too long).

TYRES

Check the tyre pressures, and inflate as necessary. Never over-inflate a tyre to try to compensate for a leak – too high a pressure not only increases tyre tread wear but also has a disastrous effect on roadholding. If a tyre's pressure has suddenly dropped to any great degree, swap it for the spare and have the leak rectified – any garage or tyre 'quick fit' centre will be able to do this. If you've never changed a wheel, take a look in chapter four, 'Flat Tyre' page 124.

Check the tyres for cuts, abrasions and bulges, and change the wheel if any such damage is visible. Check the tread wear – if it is concentrated to one side of the tyre then the tracking is out of alignment or the wheel camber is incorrect. The former can be easily adjusted at any garage and the latter indicates

Checking tyre pressures. Driving with incorrectly inflated tyres increases tyre wear greatly, it can cost you more in fuel and it most certainly reduces roadholding. Check them as frequently as you like.

If a tyre deflates this much, then have it attended to at the garage; I had purposely let the air out of the tyres, incidentally, to lower the car so that it was easier for me to spray the roof!

Spare wheel. Don't overlook the spare. If the spare in your car powers the washers, keep the pressure at 40 psi; otherwise, keep the spare pressure correct for the rear wheels (usually 26-27 psi – the glove compartment lid might sport a sticker with the tyre pressures marked on it). Carry a small tyre pressure gauge with you in the car and, if you have to use the spare, adjust the pressure accordingly. Don't use an over-inflated tyre at the front of the car – it would be dangerous to drive!

mis-set suspension – get a workshop manual or have it attended to by a professional at once, because mis-aligned suspension can give greatly reduced tyre grip (road-holding).

If tread wear is concentrated in the centre of the pattern, the tyre pressure has been too high – at both edges, too low. A tread depth gauge will enable you to check whether the depth conforms with current legislation. Fines for use of illegal tyres are very high and set to rise – in the UK at the time of writing, the fine per single illegal tyre is as high as the cost of five good quality new tyres – be warned!

UNDER THE LUGGAGE BAY LID

Lift the luggage compartment lid and check the level of the hydraulic fluid within the brake reservoir. If this suddenly drops then do not use the car on the roads until the leak has been found and rectified. If the level is slightly down, top it up. Smart people place a rag under the reservoir to catch any spillage – most brake fluids are very effective paint strippers. If you have to completely drain the hydraulic system (during a restoration or if you are to renew the fluid – an eighteen monthly job) it is worth re-filling it with silicon-based fluid which, unlike normal brake fluid, is not highly flammable,

Inflating the spare. I have a small compressor in my workshop – I'm lucky. If you have only a foot pump then you'll have to remove the spare to pump it up. Small twelve volt electric compressors for inflating tyres are inexpensive and widely available; now that many garages have started to charge for compressed air it's well worth investing in one.

Checking brake fluid level.
Note the rag stuffed under the
brake fluid reservoir to mop up
spillage. In practice, if the fluid level
drops significantly, then the car
should not be used on the road
until the cause of the leakage has
been traced and rectified.

Filling the washer bottle. Proprietary screen wash
additives seem to work well – never use washing up
liquids in the screen wash, because these can contain
salt. If the washer bottle loses pressure, suspect the
valve. Pressurise the bottle, then put a drop of moisture
in the valve opening – leakage will be apparent as bubbling. If originality is not an important issue, consider
replacing the system with a manual or electric pump.

Pressurising the washer bottle.
It's a good idea to check the washer
bottle pressure and water level
once a week.

does not absorb water, strip paintwork, nor does it need changing every eighteen months.

Still under the bonnet, check the level in the windscreen washer bottle. On early cars, the washers operate off the pressure in the spare tyre, so check that this is still 40 psi and pump it back up if necessary. On later cars, the bottle itself is pressurised, so pump it back up to 40 psi if necessary. Only on the last Beetles will you find electric screen washer motors: there are two – one for the screen, another for the headlamp washers.

INSIDE THE CAR

Nearly finished! Check the levels of the electrolyte in the battery by removing the strip or caps and looking down into each cell. If one is low then top it up using distilled water (available from any garage forecourt), but if any cells are substantially low then your battery is on the way out – change it or one morning it won't have the power to start the engine. If battery acid leakage is found, clean it all off using hot water and domestic soda – have the charging system checked by an auto-electrician, because

the battery is probably receiving too high a charge and, in time, it will boil away all the electrolyte (acid solution) and cease to function.

Finally, check that all lights, including the indicators, work, plus the horn and the windscreen wipers.

MONTHLY SERVICE

Carry out all the checks listed in the weekly service.

Like the weekly service, this comprises merely a range of checks that all is well with the car. The only extra equipment which is essential is a pair of axle stands and a bottle or small trolley jack. These don't cost a lot.

BRAKE SHOES

Engage the steering lock (where applicable) by turning the steering wheel with the ignition switched 'off'. Slacken the rear wheelnuts. Chock the front wheels, disengage the handbrake and make sure that the gearbox is in neutral, then raise the rear of the car, placing the jack (with a little wood packing) under the rear of the spine. NEVER jack up a Beetle by the

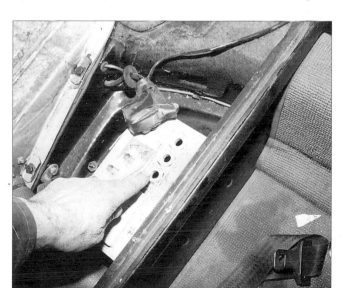

Checking battery electrolyte.
If the battery electrolyte is low, the chances are that it is being boiled off because the generator is overcharging. A voltmeter connected across the terminals with the engine running on fast tickover with or without lights, wiper motor etc. running should register 13.5-14.5 volts or thereabouts. If fifteen volts are being crammed into the battery then seek professional help.

Brake backplate with oil leakage. An MOT failure point. Oil leakage means that you need to renew the hub seals – brake fluid leakage means that the wheel cylinders need new seals. Neither job is particularly difficult nor expensive. Consult a workshop manual.

Looking inside the brake drum will confirm whether leakage is brake fluid or transaxle oil.

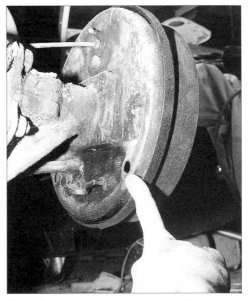

Checking brake shoe wear via inspection hole. To remove the brake drum entails tangling with the hub nut – which is torqued to a massive 253 lbs feet. To avoid you having to risk a hernia just to check brake shoe thickness, Volkswagen thoughtfully provided this inspection hole in the brake backplate. Shine a torch in here and you'll be able to see how much frictional material you have left.

engine or transaxle casing, because this can crack them. Place the axle stands under the spring plate bracket, and carefully lower the car down onto these. Check that the car is stable before proceeding.

Remove the rear road wheels. Examine the tyres for damage and tread wear. Check the flexible brake hose for damage, and inspect the brake back plates for signs of oil or hydraulic fluid leakage. There is an inspection hole in the brake backplate; remove the bung and shine a torch beam through to see the thickness of the lining. If it is approaching 0.1" (2.5mm), the shoes should be replaced at the earliest opportunity. If the handbrake has been becoming less efficient, adjust the brakes up as follows.

Remove the brake adjuster hole cover. Using

If you have to replace the brake shoes: first handbrake on, car in gear and do battle with the hub nut, then back off the brake adjusters, raise the car and support on axle stands.

a screwdriver (or a tool made by placing a small crank in the blade of an old screwdriver) through the holes in the backplate, adjust the brake by levering the star adjusters. On the off-side of the car (both front and rear brakes), the rear star of each brake should be levered upwards, the front star down, and vice-versa for the nearside of the car.

When the adjusters cannot be turned further, press the brake pedal. This centres the brake shoes, and further adjustment may be possible, followed by pressing the brake pedal again to centre the shoes. When no further adjustment is possible, back off each adjuster one notch, and turn the brake drum to ensure that the brake is not binding – if so, back off one more notch. Re-fit the road wheels and lower the car to the ground. After adjusting the handbrake, it

Remove the wheel complete with the brake drum.

A tip if you have to replace a rear hub oil seal. Press the old seal out and the new one in using a large socket in the vice. It's important that the new seal goes in square. Pack the vice jaws with wood to prevent damage.

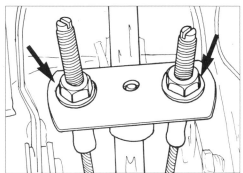

If, after the rear brakes are adjusted up, there is too much handbrake lever travel, adjust the cable ends. (*Courtesy Autodata*).

Adjusting brakes. A small flat-bladed screwdriver is OK for adjusting the brakes, though if you place a small crank about half an inch from the end you'll find it makes life easier. Wind the adjuster until the shoe makes contact with the drum (the wheel will lock), then press the brake pedal firmly to centre the shoes, and see whether further adjustment is possible. Finally, back the adjuster off one notch (to free the drum – if the brakes bind then your fuel consumption will rocket – unlike the car) and test thehandbrake. To test the hand-brake, apply it with the car rolling at a few miles per hour (don't do this on the public road). If one rear wheel locks, then only one brake is working, and the other will require further adjustment.

pays to check that it will hold the car before you drive on the road. On cars with front drum brakes, you repeat the lining checking and adjustment process.

BRAKE PADS (DISC BRAKES ONLY)

On cars fitted with front disc brakes, slacken the front wheelnuts, chock the rear wheels, jack up the front of the car and support it on axle stands. Remove the front wheels and examine the brake pad thickness (⅛" or 3mm immediately calls for renewal) and the brake

Checking brake pads. If the pads have worn too thin, you'll have to push the pistons back into the callipers in order to accommodate the new pads. It is vital that the pistons are returned square and not allowed to tip – a small strip of steel and an adjustable wrench allows you to do this.

disc for scoring, run out (spin the disc and see whether it runs true) and heat coloration. If any of these problems are found, the disc probably needs renewing. Consult a workshop manual or a repair centre.

After you've checked/adjusted the brakes, test them at low speed on your driveway if possible, before taking the car onto the road.

THERMOSTAT

Most especially in the summer, it is good policy to check that the thermostat is operating correctly. This expands as it becomes hot, operating levers which open flaps in the fan shroud, so that cool air is passed over the oil cooler radiator. If the thermostat ceases to function, the engine can overheat and eventually, seize.

Provided that the car really is stable when the rear is raised and rested on axle stands, access will be easy, although it is possible to do this with the car on its road wheels (watch out in both cases that you don't burn yourself on the hot exhaust!).

You can check the thermostat as already described using a length of stiff wire (see Weekly Checks, page 31), or you can do it 'by the book'. Remove the thermostat cover, which is held on by four self-tapping screws. Bring the engine to normal operating temperature by either driving it for a couple of miles or running it at fast tickover for about four minutes. The thermostat should have expanded to a length of 1.8" (46mm) – if not, replace it. DON'T be tempted to remove the thermostat until you have a working replacement – without the thermostat, those flaps in the fan shroud stay closed all the time!

While the rear of the car is raised, check the exhaust and heat exchangers for signs of blowing. This will be apparent as small areas of soot which, if found, indicate a need for a replacement unit. Exhaust repair materials are widely available but in reality they should be used as no more than a stop-gap measure to keep the car on the road until a new exhaust can be fitted. One sign of a leaking exhaust system, incidentally, is popping or back-firing on the overrun – if your car does this but you cannot find any evidence of a hole in the exhaust or heat exchangers, check the manifold nuts for tightness, and for leakage around the exhaust gaskets.

Finally, apply a little light oil to the door, the luggage compartment and the boot lid locks and hinges.

6 MONTH SERVICE

Unlike the previous services which consist only of a series of checks, in this service work has to be carried out. A reasonably comprehensive mechanics' toolkit will be needed, in addition to a range of spares and consumables. For the first time, the skills of the mechanic are called for, and those who don't wish to get seriously dirty should book their cars in for a 6,000 mile service – preferably at a business which specialises in working on the Beetle.

A metric socket set and spanner set is essential – always buy sockets and spanners in sets, which works out far cheaper than buying them individually (the same usually applies to other tools such as screwdrivers, pliers and mole grips). Choose a socket set with ½" drive rather than a ⅜" drive which is too puny for some of the work, and both sockets and spanners will be needed from 6mm to 22mm.

A good jack and axle stands are also essential. You will also need a set of feeler gauges, spark plug spanner (there should be one with the socket set), a set of straight and Philips-headed screwdrivers, pliers, side cutters, grease gun and, if you wish to check and adjust the ignition timing yourself (optional in the six month service, essential annually), a stroboscopic timing light.

You will need engine and transaxle oil in the correct grade, lithium-based grease, an oil strainer and plug gasket, rocker box cover gaskets and, depending on the condition of these components, you may require points, spark plugs and a generator drive belt. You won't know exactly what is needed until you have inspected the various components, and so a quick pre-service check will enable you to acquire necessary spares before you start the service proper.

Distributor cap. Press on the centre of each spring clip in turn and pull the top off the ledge in the distributor cap. Not much fun when your hands are cold!

Points and condenser. The condenser should be renewed along with the points, because excessive burning of the points is most frequently due to a failed condenser. It is worth buying an 'ignition service kit' rather than buying points, plugs etc. individually – there is always a worthwhile saving, and you might discover that one of the mail order spares specialists happens to have service kits on special offer.

INSPECTION

Remove the distributor cap by pressing simultaneously on both clip centres and pulling off the ends. Check the mating surfaces of the points for burning or an uneven surface (pitting) and, if the points are pitted, acquire a new set of points and a condenser before starting the service proper (the reason the points are burning is that the condenser is not doing its job – see chapter four for an explanation).

Remove the sparking plugs and check their condition. If the electrode has burned away to any extent then acquire a new set of plugs. If the electrodes are covered with black soot then make a note to later weaken or have weakened the fuel/air mixture, because the engine is running too rich (see chapter four). If the plug

Checking plug gap. As the electrode burns away, the plug gap can increase to the point at which only a weak spark occurs when you're trying in vain to start the engine from cold on full choke – when it needs a good, strong spark to ignite the rich (fifteen times as much petrol as used in normal running) mixture.

electrodes are covered with a sticky black layer, the engine is burning oil (this has either come past the piston oil control rings or down the valve stem to guide gap – sooner or later the engine or cylinder head will need overhauling). If the plugs have a glazed appearance then the engine is running very hot which, as already stated, requires immediate attention to avert possible damage to the engine (check that the thermostat is functioning correctly). Glazed spark plugs should be discarded and replaced. The plug electrodes should be a light fawn colour and, if this proves to be the case, check their gaps now while they are out of the engine. The gap should be 0.23" (0.6mm).

In addition, carry out all of the other checks listed to date.

GENERATOR DRIVE BELT ADJUSTMENT

To adjust the belt, lock the generator by inserting a screwdriver into the slot in the front pulley so that its end rests against one of the screws in the casing, then slacken the large (21mm) pulley nut. Tightening the belt

involves removing one of the shims from in between the two halves of the pulley (replace it under the nut – you'll need to replace it in between the two pulley halves when you come to fit a new belt), then reassembling the pulley and tightening the nut. The pulley nut should

Adjusting generator drive belt tension. To tighten the belt, remove a washer, reassemble, re-check, and remove a further washer if necessary

Adjusting generator drive belt tension. To adjust the generator drive belt tension, firstly lock the generator with a screwdriver as shown, then slacken the nut. This has been torqued to 43 lbs ft, so you'll need to use a bit of muscle.

Place the washers you remove on the outside of the pulley under the nut – when the time comes to fit a new (un-stretched) drive belt, you will have to replace those washers in between the pulley halves.

Tightening the pulley nut. If you don't possess a torque wrench, buy one – they're a good investment. Tighten the nut to 43 lbs ft. The correct way to use a torque wrench is to slacken the nut slightly, then to tighten it up in one smooth movement. If you try to use a torque wrench on an already tightened nut, friction can give you a false reading. Do not use modern super lubricants on any thread which is to be torqued – the reduced friction can easily allow you to over-tighten and consequently damage the thread. Use only ordinary engine oil on threads which are to be tightened with a torque wrench.

be torqued to 43 lbs ft – if you don't possess a torque wrench, borrow one. Re-check the tension and, if necessary, remove another shim.

STEERING BOX

I always take the opportunity to check and adjust the steering box every six months. With the front wheels pointing dead ahead, turn a steering wheel a little one way then the other, noting whether there is very much 'void' travel – that is, movement at the steering wheel perimeter which does not turn the front wheels. If there is much more than ½", you'll need a 17mm ring spanner, small cross head and larger straight bladed screwdrivers. Remove the spare wheel, and you'll note two covers screwed onto the back of the spare wheel compartment. Remove the one on the

same side of the car as the steering wheel. Slacken the large nut which surrounds a screw head, then turn the screw clockwise until slight resistance is felt. Re-check the steering wheel movement and, if the void travel has disappeared, hold the screw head whilst pinching up the 17mm nut – just like adjusting a valve. Use the steering wheel to turn the front wheels from lock to lock and, if the steering becomes heavy at full lock, you've over-tightened the screw, so check this and slacken it off a fraction if necessary.

ENGINE OIL CHANGE

You need a receptacle to catch the old engine oil, and a plastic five litre oil container with a large hole cut in one side is ideal. Any garage can dispose of old engine oil for you – don't throw it down the drain.

Place the receptacle under the drain plug and unscrew the plug – wear disposable plastic gloves because oil is not good for your skin – and allow the 4.4 pints of oil to drain. To quicken the draining, remove the oil filler cap. When the engine oil has apparently finished draining, remove the oil strainer cover bolts, the strainer cover and assembly, wash the lot in neat petrol (keep this well away from any possible source of ignition, such as a heater or any naked flame), dry it thoroughly and re-fit both the strainer assembly and oil drain plug along with new gaskets.

The engine now requires 4.4 pints of clean new engine oil. The Beetle oil filler cap is awkwardly placed, and re-filling is best accomplished by metering oil out into a thin-necked (thin enough to fit inside the filler neck) one pint container, which is offered up to the filler neck and quickly tipped up. This allows you to accurately meter out the 4.4 pints.

Before leaving this subject, it is worth mentioning a tip from Terry Ball of Beetle Specialist Workshop. Terry prefers to fill the engine with 4.4 pints of diesel oil, to run the engine ON TICKOVER for a minute or so, and then

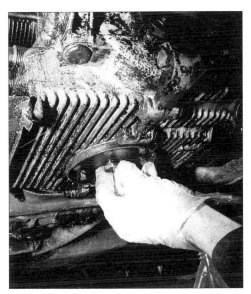

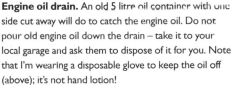

Engine oil drain. An old 5 litre oil container with one side cut away will do to catch the engine oil. Do not pour old engine oil down the drain – take it to your local garage and ask them to dispose of it for you. Note that I'm wearing a disposable glove to keep the oil off (above); it's not hand lotion!

Do make sure that the container is properly positioned to catch the oil. I was so concerned with trying to take the photo (above right) that I managed to get an oil slick on the workshop floor. Sawdust is as good as anything, incidentally, for soaking up spillages like this.

Cleaning the oil strainer. Wash the strainer in neat petrol (right); take all precautions against setting this on fire – no electrical devices or naked flames in the vicinity. If you find a yellow-ochre gunge in the filler neck then this is an emulsion of oil and water (condensation) most frequently found in cars which are used predominantly for short trips – clean it out and check that the breather is not blocked.

to drain the diesel before filling the engine with new engine oil. This does help clean out the engine and more importantly the oil cooler radiator. An alternative to actually running the engine would be to whip out the spark plugs, disconnect the HT lead from the coil and spin the engine on the starter motor for perhaps two periods of ten seconds' duration – your battery, of course, would have to be in good order and fully charged. This would avoid subjecting the big end bearings to the pounding they get with the engine running if they happened to be reasonably worn, but would flush the diesel oil right around the system and clean away sludge.

I personally make a point of spinning the engine on the starter as just described immediately after filling the engine with new oil. This builds up oil pressure and gets oil into the important areas of the engine before it is subjected to the stresses of actually firing up.

I know I'm repeating myself, but discarded DIY mechanics' old engine oil is a major pollutant; never throw this down the drain or bury it, but take it to your nearest service centre, where it will be collected for recycling.

BRAKES

Check shoe and/or pad lining thickness, and replace if necessary. Adjust the rear brakes, then adjust the cables at the handbrake lever end so that the lever rises four notches before locking the rear brakes. Whilst the front of the car is raised to enable you to check the front brakes, give the torsion bar assembly grease nipples a few strokes with a grease gun.

Greasing the torsion bar. Something which is easily overlooked.

TRANSAXLE

Check the drive shaft boots/gaiters (depending on whether the car is swing axle or trailing arm) for leakage, and replace or have them replaced if necessary.

The transaxle oil level is often neglected by Beetle owners, with the result that the inspection hole plug becomes very reluctant to move.

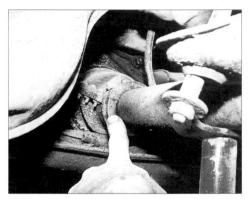

Drive shaft boots. Oil leakage from the drive shaft boots is an MOT failure point – it's not terribly good for the transaxle, either! New boots come in two halves, and aren't difficult to fit. Unless you want an oil slick on your workshop floor, place a receptacle underneath the old boot to catch the oil.

Transaxle oil plug tool. One sure and regrettably frequent sign of skimped maintenance is a seized transaxle oil filler plug. I made up a tool for removing this plug by welding a cut-down 17mm headed bolt onto a lever; two nuts locked together on a bolt would have the same effect. If the plug is really seized, however, go to your nearest garage and beg the use of a 17mm hexagonal drive.

When tracing the source of oil leakage, check out the pushrod tube ends – prime suspects.

There are special tools available for this purpose, and on the worst seized examples nothing short of a sturdy hexagonal drive and a large spanner will do, although a 17mm headed bolt, either welded to a lever or with two nuts locked tightly together and driven by a spanner will suffice provided the plug is not too tight.

Remove the plug. The oil level should reach the lower edge of the plug hole, and so it is important to ensure that the car is on level ground when making this check. If necessary, top up with Hypoid SAE 90 gear oil, and take the time to find and cure the leak.

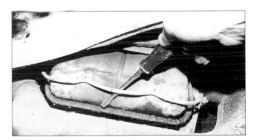

Prising off rocker box cover springs. Working whilst lying on your back with flakes of rust and underseal dropping into your eyes is no-one's idea of fun. When working under the car, wear some form of eye protection.

VALVE CLEARANCES

Chock the front wheels, raise the rear of the car and support it on axle stands – make sure it is stable before proceeding. Select neutral gear. Remove the HT leads from the spark plugs, then remove the spark plugs to make it possible for you to turn the engine over by hand. The engine should be cold. Clean as best you can the accumulated muck from the rocker box covers and the surrounding area. Remove the spring clips and rocker box covers to reveal the valve gear.

Remove the distributor cap. Using a spanner on the generator pulley nut, turn the engine over until the rotor arm is pointing to the position of the number one spark plug terminal (and at the small notch in the distributor body rim), at which time the notch in the crankshaft pulley should be pointing upwards and be in line with the crankcase joint line or, if there are two notches, slightly to the right of it – for a full description of how to decipher Beetle crankshaft pulley timing marks, see 'Ignition

Setting valve gaps. The principle is simple; check the gap with a feeler gauge and, if adjustment proves necessary, slacken the locknut, adjust the ball-end screw until the feeler gauge is lightly gripped then hold the screw steady as you re-tighten the nut. One problem with high mileage engines is that the rocker pads wear into a concave section, which makes it difficult to accurately set the gap – 'click-adjust' type tools overcome this minor difficulty.

Timing', below. Insert a 0.006" (0.15mm) feeler gauge between the rockers and valve stems of number one cylinder (offside of the car nearest the front).

It should enter and move with just a little resistance. If it is slack or tight, the valve will have to be adjusted. To do this, slacken the locknut with a ring spanner whilst holding the screw still with a screwdriver, tighten the screw a fraction until the feeler gauge can be moved but offer slight resistance, then hold the screw in this position and pinch up the locknut. This takes a bit of practice, but you soon get the hang of it.

Turn the crankshaft anti-clockwise through 180°, check that the rotor arm is now pointing at the position usually occupied by number two HT terminal, and check the clearances of number two cylinder valve gear (offside rear). Turn the crankshaft through 180° again, and check the valve clearances of number three cylinder (which is nearside front), and finally repeat for number four.

If the engine is stone cold, a quicker method is to turn the crankshaft until the pulley notch is at top dead centre (TDC). On one cylinder head, three rockers will be slack and one tight; on the other three will be tight and one slack. Adjust the valve clearances for the slack rockers. Turn the crankshaft through 360° (one

complete turn). The rockers which were previously tight will now be slack – adjust these.

CONTACT BREAKER POINTS

You should have checked the condition of the points in your pre-service inspection; if new points have to be fitted, simply remove the screw which secures the point to the base plate, disconnect the low tension lead, then pull the old points out and fit the new ones. The points gap has to be altered (if the existing points are retained, the points gap should of course be checked).

Turn the engine over until the points' heel rests on a cam lobe, so that the points are fully open. Place a 0.016" (0.4mm) feeler gauge in between the points; it should enter and move with just a little resistance. If the gap is too large or small, slacken the securing screw and adjust the gap using a screwdriver blade lodged in the baseplate notch, then tighten the screw and re-test.

IGNITION TIMING

Note: Beetles with fuel injection should be dynamically timed using a stroboscope.

Whenever you have adjusted the points gap, you should follow up by adjusting the ignition timing. There are two methods of doing this; static and dynamic. Static timing requires no

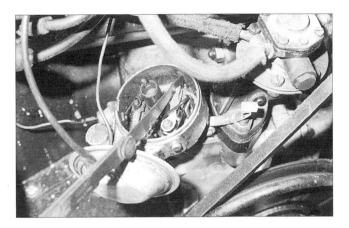

Feeler gauge in points gap. The heel is situated on a cam lobe, which opens the points to their fullest extent. The feeler gauge can then be inserted.

Adjusting points gap. Slacken the base locking screw, and adjust as shown. Always remember to re-set the ignition timing after altering the points gap.

Crank pulley – timing marks. If, after reading the text, you're still not sure which pulley mark represents what degrees and what your engined should be timed at, go to a service centre and ask a mechanic to adjust the timing and make a mark for you. Even if you are fairly certain you've located the right mark, there's always an outside chance that a previous owner fitted a non-standard pulley.

specialised tools, but is not as accurate as dynamic timing, which requires the use of a stroboscope. Stroboscopic timing lights can be acquired at fairly low prices, and are well worth having (for dynamic timing, you'll also need a bottle of typists' correction fluid, or some white paint and a small brush).

The timing marks on some Beetles are a nightmare to sort out! Because of this, it might be appropriate to have the timing set professionally at first. Modern professional garage equipment allows the operator to set the timing given only TDC, and the exhaustive tune-up literature at the disposal of professionals covers virtually all of the vehicles on the road. If the mechanic makes a mark on the pulley then make this permanent using a centre punch as soon as you get back home! You can alternatively – where necessary – find your own timing mark using a protractor.

Most Beetle engines are timed at 7.5 degrees BTDC, some at 5 degrees, one at 10 and some at top dead centre; if the crankshaft pulley has just one notch, then this represents the correct timing mark for all Beetles, *except for* 1300s made after October 1971, on which the mark signifies 0 degrees (TDC). If the crank pulley has two marks, use the one on the left (7.5 degrees – the other is 10 degrees) *Except for* 1200s with an engine serial number between 5000000 and 9725086, which are 10 degrees BTDC (use the right-hand mark).

Some Beetle crank pulleys have three marks, and this is where things get complicated; 1600 B series engines are 0 degrees (left-hand mark), 1500s are 7.5 degrees (centre mark) except for H series between 087928 and 1124670, which are 0 degrees (left hand mark). On 1200 engines the marks represent 0, 7.5 and 10 degrees, with 0 far left; D series between 0675000 and 1268062 are 0 degrees, engines between 5000000 and 9725086 are 10 degrees. Like I said, a nightmare! But this is complicated by the fact that your Beetle might not necessarily, for whatever reason, be fitted with the

correct crankshaft pulley, or, it might have been fitted with a different distributor, which also throws the timing marks out. For this reason, it is strongly recommended that you have the timing set professionally on Sun or Crypton equipment, and ask the mechanic to make the correct timing mark on the crank pulley for future reference.

One welcome bonus of putting your Beetle onto this sort of equipment is its ability to highlight other problems such as worn distributor bearings, electrical losses in the ignition circuit, or carburation problems – any of which can adversely affect performance or economy and which the amateur is not likely to discover for him or her self.

STATIC TIMING – CARBURETTOR BEETLES

Remove the distributor cap, plug leads, and plugs. Turn the engine over using a spanner on the generator pulley nut until the rotor arm is pointing at the position occupied by the number one HT lead terminal (it will also be pointing at the small notch in the distributor body). Turn the engine anti-clockwise until the split or

Static timing. Rotor arm in line with the tiny notch in the distributor body rim and pulley timing marks aligned. You now have to turn the distributor body so that the contact breaker points open at this precise part of the cycle.

Static timing. If you connect a light bulb across the points with the ignition switched on, it will illuminate at the exact moment the points separate. Alternatively, turn on the car radio and tune it off station – it will crackle as the points begin to separate. Here, I've connected a meter (ignition switched off) across the points. It is set to read resistance and, when the points separate, the needle swings sharply from one side of the dial to the other. Line up the crank pulley timing mark, slacken the base clamp bolt, turn the distributor body until the points are just starting to open, then re-tighten the base clamp bolt.

Dynamic timing. Stroboscope timing lights don't cost a lot. Some strobes emit more light than others, though, and if you find that yours is fairly dim then you'll have to park the car somewhere shaded so that you can see the illuminated timing marks! Find the right timing mark on the crank pulley, highlight this with a dab of Typex or white paint, connect the strobe to No.1 spark plug and its lead, and away you go! Watch out that you don't get the strobe wires entangled in the generator drive belt.

appropriate mark in the crankcase is aligned with the appropriate timing notch in the crankshaft pulley. At this point in the crank rotation the points should just be starting to open. To check this, connect a 12V bulb across the points – ignition switched on – and it will light the instant that the points begin to separate. Alternatively, turn the car radio on and tune it just off-channel – a crack will be heard from the speaker as the points separate. To adjust the timing, slacken the base clamp bolt and rotate the distributor body.

DYNAMIC TIMING

The remarks concerning those years and models of Beetles which have only TDC marked on the flywheel pulley apply equally for dynamic timing.

Use typists' correction fluid or a small dab of white paint to highlight the timing marks, which makes them more visible under the light of the strobe. Disconnect the HT lead from number one spark plug, and connect one lead from the strobe to the plug, and the other to its HT lead.

Every time that the plug fires, the strobe is illuminated for a very short space of time, sufficient to make any moving object illuminated by it – in this case, the timing marks – appear stationary. Disconnect the vacuum advance pipe from the distributor, and blank off the end of the pipe (otherwise you'll have a weak mixture). Ensure that none of the leads can become entangled in the generator drive belt. Start the engine, then shine the strobe light onto the crankshaft pulley. If there is too much extraneous light (on a very bright day), you'll have to arrange or find some sort of shade to work in if you are to see the timing marks.

The motion of the crankshaft pulley will appear to be arrested by the flashing strobe light, and if the two marks do not align, turn the ignition off, slacken the distributor body bolt, and turn the distributor one way or the other to alter the timing. Anti-clockwise to advance the timing and vice-versa. When the two marks appear adjacent, tighten the distributor bolt.

STATIC AND DYNAMIC TIMING

After setting ther timing it is good policy to take the car for a run and to try to ascend a slope on a light throttle setting; if the engine pinks (a tinkling sound which is actually the pistons tipping in their bores and which – if not corrected – will eventually wreck the engine), retard the ignition timing slightly.

Sluggish response and a drop in performance suggests that the timing is too far retarded; but pinking or – worse – knocking when laden with a light throttle setting suggests that the timing is too far advanced. (Pinking and especially knocking can damage the engine in a short space of time, so retard the ignition at once!).

SETTING THE MIXTURE – FUEL INJECTION

It is strongly recommended that any adjustments to the fuel injection system are carried out professionally by a company which possesses the appropriate equipment and preferably one which specialises in the Beetle.

SETTING THE MIXTURE – CARBURETTORS

There is a strong case for having this work carried out professionally, because modern garage equipment allows it to be done very accurately and can discover faults which adversely affect performance or fuel consumption and which

Adjusting mixture. There is a strong case for having the mixture set at a garage using exhaust analysing gear. At MOT test centres, this is built into diagnostic equipment which can reveal any problems with the ignition, so have the ignition checked and set, then ask them to adjust the mixture. Small DIY exhaust gas analysers are widely available and, in my experience, quite accurate.

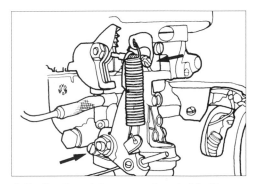

Adjusting the mixture on earlier models. Once the mixture has been accurately set, don't be tempted to keep tinkering with it! (Courtesy Autodata).

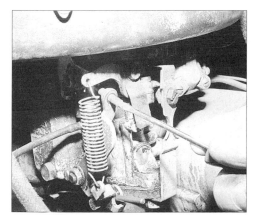

Adjusting idle speed. Don't be tempted to raise the tickover speed to compensate for rough idling – you'll end up using a lot more petrol! Again, modern professional engine diagnostic equipment can trace the fault which causes the rough tickover.

Meter. Some DIY multi-meters can show the engine revolutions and allow you to set tickover precisely. However, the Beetle owner should be familiar enough with the sound of an engine to be able to set tickover revolutions by ear!

DIY methods are unlikely to uncover. Alternatively, small DIY emissions testers are not too expensive to buy and are, in my experience, quite accurate enough for the job.

However, that said, the mixture can be set reasonably accurately at home without specialised equipment, provided that everything is in first-class working order and that the ignition is set spot-on.

Bring the engine to normal working temperature, then turn the throttle adjusting screw until the tickover revs rise to 1,000 rpm or thereabouts – in effect, a fast tickover. Screw in the mixture control screw until the engine starts to run a little erratically, then back the screw off by one-third of a turn (60 degrees). Then re adjust the tickover back down to 750-850 rpm.

ANNUAL SERVICE

Carry out all of the checks and jobs detailed thus far. It is good policy in addition to renew the contact breaker points, condenser, distributor cap and leads and spark plugs – these components can often be bought as an 'ignition service kit' at lower prices than they would be available separately. Also renew the air filter, engine breather filter and fuel line filter (where fitted).

I prefer to time the annual service so that it coincides with MOT testing time – that way, it doesn't get overlooked. Carrying out a full annual service before submitting the car for the MOT test also greatly increases your chances of finding and being able to rectify faults, and hence the chances of the car passing the test first-time. Pay attention to detail; most MOT test failures are due to silly little faults such as a depleted windscreen washer bottle or a blown light bulb.

Something else MOT testers do is discover faults, the rectification of which will usually be described – step by step – in a full workshop manual, but which are really beyond the scope of a book like this – problems like a damaged

Air filter clean, oil fill. Later cars have a straightforward replaceable element air filter, earlier cars use this oil bath affair. Slacken the slot-head bolts on the filter clamp and the bracket which points down-wards, then lift off the filter body. It is not necessary to remove the engine bay lid – I did that to make the photography easier! Don't over-fill the filter.

Bleeding drum brake. Bleeding the brakes usually goes without a hitch – occasionally, it will prove one of the most frustrating things you can attempt on a car. Do remember to keep topping up the master cylinder – bleed this dry and you will be obliged to bleed the entire system!

Bleeding disc brake. Rather than use the traditional jam jar with fluid inside, I drilled a hole in an old brake fluid container lid, so that the pipe is a snug fit. This lessens the chances of spilling brake fluid all over the place, and a plastic container is obviously preferable to glass.

brake or fuel line, worn wheel bearings and so on. Don't curse the MOT tester who discovers some such fault with your car – these faults compromise safety – in this case, it's yours! Thank them for their vigilance, get hold of a workshop manual or have the work carried out professionally.

EVERY EIGHTEEN MONTHS

As six-monthly service, but also renew the brake fluid. If you use a modern silicon fluid, it won't need replacing again. Check the brake flexible hoses and replace if damaged. Check all steering/suspension fittings for tightness.

EVERY THREE YEARS

As annual plus eighteen month service, but renew the brake master cylinder and wheel cylinder seals. Check the cylinders for scoring or corrosion and replace or hone as necessary. Renew the brake flexible hoses.

PASS THE MOT(UK)

PRE-MOT CHECK-OVER

This section is written for the non-technically minded, and deals with finding those seemingly trivial faults which commonly lead to easily avoidable MOT failures. Vehicle testing criteria will vary from country to country (seek local professional advice), though most will include the tests listed here.

Firstly, never leave your car at a testing station with the instructions that whatever work proves necessary for the MOT test should be attended to. This is tantamount to saying 'Here's a signed cheque with the amount left blank – have a nice day'.

Let's kick off with the MOT failure points which are so obvious to spot and so simple to rectify that you'll kick yourself if your car fails on any of them. The only way to be certain that you spot faults is to do what the MOT tester will do, to follow his routine.

The first thing the MOT tester usually does is to sit in the driver's seat and tug on the seat belt webbing to check the mountings, so do

Brake wheel cylinder stripped. Master and wheel cylinder problems can usually be cured in one of two ways. Fit a new cylinder (expensive), or acquire a seal kit, strip (and, if necessary, hone) the cylinder and rebuild it. Any workshop manual will describe this work in detail.

this, and if you manage to pull one free then you're probably sitting in a rotten car! Check that the belts themselves are not frayed (a failure in the UK), and that the inertia mechanism (where fitted) works. Rock both seats to ensure that they are securely mounted.

Examine the windscreen for cracks or chips: the rules governing what is and what is not acceptable and what may and may not be repaired are rather complicated (the British Standards code of practice for windscreen repair is allegedly not entirely in agreement with MOT regs) so seek professional advice if you discover any problems with the windscreen. Remove any window stickers if there is the slightest chance that the tester could deem them to obstruct the driver's vision. Check that the sun visors and rear view mirror are secure (and hence won't suddenly drop down). Check that the doors open and shut properly (and thus cannot fly open when the car is on the move).

Operate the windscreen washers and ensure that both jets strike the screen half way up (also check that there's plenty of water in the washer reservoir immediately before setting out for the test). Then operate the wiper blades to check that they sweep the screen clear. Check that the horn works – this is important if, like me, you can go a full year without venting your 'road rage' on the horn button – it could have packed up months ago and I wouldn't know!

Grab the steering wheel and pull and push it to feel for play in the flange joint or one of the universal joints (MacPherson strut cars). Then open the door so that you can see the front wheel and turn the steering wheel first one way then the other, checking the amount by which the steering wheel perimeter moves before the front wheel begins to turn (this varies according to the size of the steering wheel but as a rough guide, more than an inch will usually mean an MOT failure – if in doubt, ask before you book your car in for the test).

With the aid of an assistant, check that all elements of the lighting system are functional – indicators (hazard warning, reversing and fog/spot lamps if fitted), side lights, rear number plate light, headlamps (main beam and dipped) and stop lights.

Lift the engine bay lid and check visually that there are no damaged wires, no fuel leakage or un-insulated connectors.

Remove the fuel filler cap and check that the rubber sealing gasket is intact. Check the tyres for correct inflation and check the tightness of the wheelnuts. Visually examine the wiper blades for damage, wear or perishing through old age.

'Bounce' each corner of the car (press downwards and allow the suspension to push the body back up) to check that the dampers are functional. The body should rise, fall a little then settle. If the body comes back up then goes back down and so on then the dampers will fail the test.

The checks covered so far take just a few minutes to carry out and, if your car passes them, you will have eliminated some of the most common MOT failure points. If you wish to carry out further checks, you're going to

Steering box. Pre-MacPherson cars have a steering box, and play in the steering (usually discovered at MOT time) can be taken up by slackening off the lock nut, screwing in the adjuster (steering dead ahead – don't over-tighten) and tightening the lock nut. If the steering becomes tight at full lock, you've overdone it.

have to get dirty. You will need a jack – use a bottle or trolley jack and not a scissors jack – wheel chocks and a pair of axle stands. Apply chocks to whichever wheels are to remain on the ground when the car is raised. When you have raised the car, support it on axle stands before carrying out any of the checks listed here.

With the car raised as necessary, check the tyres carefully for tread depth, bulges and damage. Whilst each side of the car is raised, use a pointed piece of hardwood to prod fairly vigorously at the heater channels and the areas around the rear body and bumper mounting points – if you manage to poke a hole then major surgery is called for. The MOT tester will use a Ministry regulation hammer which might appear to be too puny to break toffee but which is fully capable of smashing a hole in rotten steel pressings.

Raise the front of the car and support it on axle stands. Spin each front wheel and listen for wheel bearing roughness. Grab each front tyre in turn top and bottom, then push and pull to find any play which – whatever the cause –

Spinning wheel. While the front wheel is off the ground, spin it and listen for roughness in the wheel bearings – not to be confused with disc binding; if you can't tell which is which, bring in help.

Turn the wheel from lock to lock to listen for roughness in the steering rack, and feel for damper problems, amongst others.

means a failure. Turn a front wheel from lock to lock, listening for roughness in the steering rack or box, and noting whether there is any play – which could be due to the steering rack, steering box or the track rod ends. Also, feel for constant resistance from the steering damper (where fitted), which might be apparent as a part of the travel where the resistance suddenly disappears.

Whilst the front of the car is raised and using a torch to improve illumination, check that the steering rack gaiters are not damaged or leaking, and visually examine all of the bushes in the suspension of the car – if any are perished, expect a failure.

Visually check for leakage from the dampers and the brake hydraulic system. Check the condition of brake lines and flexible hoses, and check that the hoses of the front brakes don't

foul the wheel with the steering at full lock. At the rear of the car, check for brake fluid or axle oil leakage on the brake backplates, and leakage from the drive shaft gaiters.

PROBLEM AREAS

There are some components of the test which you cannot 100% guarantee your car will pass unless you possess specialised equipment to check headlight alignment, braking efficiency and exhaust emissions, so we'll deal with these as best we can.

Have the headlight alignment set professionally, then drive back to your garage. Park about ten to fifteen feet away from your garage door (or a wall if you don't have a garage – measure and record the distance in either case), switch on the headlights (both full and dipped beam) and paint marks on the door where the beams strike. Provided that your tyre pressures were correct when you made the marks, you can now check your headlight vertical adjustment at will.

That is about as far as you can go without getting seriously dirty and, even if you only carry out the checks covered so far, you will have eliminated what in practice probably make up the majority of MOT failure points. If you wish to go further then I strongly recommend that alongside these brief guidlines you refer to a good workshop manual.

The braking efficiency at the individual wheel is difficult to check. What you can do is raise each wheel from the ground in turn and try to turn it whilst the hand or foot brake is applied as appropriate. If you are unable to shift the wheel then this unfortunately proves nothing; but if you can turn it then you're looking at an MOT failure for sure!

Handbrake deficiencies due to poor adjustment account for many an MOT failure. As a conscientious owner, you will naturally have attended to the rear brake adjusters on a regular basis so that they will not be seized. This being the case, raise the rear of the car (remove the roadwheels if you wish) and see whether there is scope for adjustment.

Wind up each adjuster until it stops, then apply the foot brake to centre the brake shoes, and see whether the adjuster can be persuaded to turn a little further. Check that the brakes don't drag.

Exhaust emission tests can be carried out at home if you splash out on one of the recently introduced DIY testers (such as the Gunson's Gastester which, in my limited experience, is quite accurate enough for the purpose). In the absence of such a machine, the best advice is to check the ignition system – contact breaker points condition, gap and – if you possess an automotive multi-meter – dwell angle, the spark plug gaps and condition, high tension leads and connections. If all is well then you should have a good strong spark at the plugs and (assuming the engine is in good condition), in the knowledge that high CO_2 emission must therefore be down to the carburation, you can ask the mechanic to check and if necessary set this before starting the MOT test.

The emissions test for older cars is a visual one – they should not belch smoke from the exhaust – and you can obviously check this for yourself.

Other checks which you can make include the air filter (paper element type only – a blocked filter will enrich the mixture), and that the choke mechanism is not sticking, which would give too rich a mixture.

Bear in mind that no-one can guarantee a first-time MOT pass – the tester might spot something one day which he might miss on another, and the regulations are open to some degree of interpretation – one tester might fail a car which another would pass. By carrying out the checks listed above, you do increase your chances of getting a pass certificate, and certainly guard against failing on some silly, trivial point.

PROFESSIONAL MAINTENANCE

If you entrust the maintenance of your Beetle to a garage, it is as well to carry out all the simple weekly and monthly checks at home, which will not only ensure that your Beetle remains fully fit for the road but also give you a gentle introduction to maintenance – perhaps when you feel a little braver, you'll try carrying out the six monthly and other servicing.

The Beetle is an old car and, unlike new cars, it is difficult to set hard and fast service intervals and to know which jobs should be tackled religiously at those intervals. It is, therefore, a good idea to discuss exactly what work you think needs doing and any extra suggested with the mechanic who will actually do the work, rather than with a service manager. When you speak to the mechanic you have the opportunity to inform him or her of any little observations which you feel need looking into – an occasional misfire or cold/hot starting problems, for instance. If you cannot get to speak to the mechanic then I suggest you take your car elsewhere.

If the same mechanic services your Beetle every time, then he or she gets to know you and the car and – equally importantly – they will know which items will need checking and which jobs need doing. A good mechanic will, when working on an older car, keep an eye out for any developing problems rather than unthinkingly going through the motions of the service routine and, by bringing these to your attention, can save you the trauma of an on-road breakdown.

Before commissioning any work, do check what the workshop hourly rate is; some garages charge many times as much as others. Large modern service centres will always have much higher overheads than smaller businesses, and what the smaller outfit lacks in expensive sophisticated equipment (which – fuel injected cars excepted – isn't needed for Beetle maintenance) it can make up for in attention to detail. I would personally avoid large franchised garages, because the mechanics here tend to work on newish cars and won't have the same sort of experience of working on old cars that the mechanics employed at a small garage will. If there is a Beetle specialist within reasonable travelling distance, then this is always the best option.

I'm afraid that certain sections of the motor trade have a diabolical reputation for ripping the customer off, and a few precautions will help prove whether work and parts charged for have actually been carried out/fitted. A bottle of typists' correction fluid can be used to mark nuts and bolts which should be undone, such as the generator pulley thread. If this is disturbed but you see on the bill that you are being charged for adjusting the generator drive belt tension, you know that you're being ripped off and you should look elsewhere for further skullduggery. Items which should be replaced such as spark plugs, the distributor cap or high tension leads can be discreetly marked. There is no guarantee that you can catch out every little dodge which has been employed by the cowboy element of the trade; obtaining a good workshop manual does, however, tell you exactly which jobs should be carried out and give you a fighting chance of uncovering attempts to rip you off.

Don't automatically assume that a mechanic is going to try to pull a fast one, and never give the impression that you distrust the mechanic because most of them are honest and hard-working types who appreciate being shown a little consideration by customers. Every car mechanic has to deal with awkward and inconsiderate customers. Every mechanic experiences – on a daily basis – customers who, the day after having a new hub oil seal or a set of brake shoes fitted to their car, come in to complain loudly and at length that they've lost synchro on third gear "AND IT WAS ALL RIGHT BEFORE *YOU* TOUCHED IT". The unreasonable customer is not, sadly, in the minority – most people treat car mechanics pretty badly. Show the mechanic a little respect and he'll treat you like royalty.

LOOK AFTER YOUR BODY

Washing the car regularly not only keeps it looking good, but also – if you thoroughly swill and brush out accumulated mud from the underside and within the wheelarches – keeps rust at bay. Begin by hosing all mud from inside the wheelarches and under the running boards/heater channel areas (use a broom to loosen the really tenacious stuff), then wash the bodywork, starting at the top and working down. Never use household washing up liquids on your car – they contain industrial salts – use only proper car shampoo and, if you want the paintwork to keep shining, follow that up with car wax. The modern colour enriched waxes can brighten up jaded paintwork no end.

Cheap bumpers rust in double quick time. Pin-holes of rust surrounded by staining are already on the surface of my bumpers after a year, and here I'm using a mild cutting liquid to remove the surface stains before treating the bumpers to hard wax protection. This won't slow the rusting, but removing the surface stain makes the car look a little smarter for now.

Underneath the car, it is a good idea to periodically (say annually, before the onset of Winter) use a pressure washer, which not only blasts off mud, but also any loose underseal, giving you the opportunity to clean rust off the newly exposed steel, to paint and re-underseal it. I prefer to whip off the running boards and wings every couple of years, scrape the rust and what remains of the paint from the undersides and re-paint them. Not only does this extend the life of the wings and running boards, it also allows you to put some fresh grease onto the fixing bolts – leave these alone for a few years

and the chances are they'll be seized when you do try to get them off. While I'm doing this, I take the opportunity to paint a little engine oil onto the inside of the running board chrome strips – and you can do the same for the strips on the car's sides.

In addition, whenever you use a grease gun and surplus grease oozes out of the component concerned, scoop it up and wipe it onto any nearby ferrous surfaces – for instance, when you grease the torsion bar, always wipe the surplus onto the frame head – it's an effective rust preventative.

Stone chip paint. The lower leading edges of the rear wings are especially prone to stone chipping. You can feather the edge of the stone chip paint once it has hardened to lose the hard edge. Don't make the same mistake I previously have – namely, spraying cellulose over the stone chip paint before this had fully hardened. If you do, then the topcoat will almost certainly crack open. If this happens, clean out the cracks with spirit wipe, use body stopper to fill the cracks up, wet flat the entire area and re-paint.

Waxes and similar anti-rust products are the most popular way to keep enclosed box-sections topside from rusting. The door skins and their bases (don't block the drain holes), the inside of the quarter panel – anywhere that water might condense out and cause rusting to commence.

To fully protect your Beetle using a wax or similar product (a friend swears by a mixture of proprietary wax and old sump oil, applied using a compressor and underseal gun; another friend rates old sump oil mixed with creosote – I prefer waxes), begin at one end of the car and work your way to the other. At the front, the rear of the front panel, the insides of the headlight bowls and down the insides of the A posts can all be reached using a proprietary wax applicator with a long nozzle. Inside the car in the front lower edge of the A post you'll find a small hole, which is there to help you guide the heater pipe down onto the heater channel outlet – apply lots of wax through here, because both the A post and heater channels rot.

Still inside the car, whip off the door and rear side panels and apply plenty of wax inside the door and on the rear of the quarter panel. Take out the rear seat base as well and you should be able to get some wax up around the tops of the wheelarches and, of course, you can treat the area under the seat.

If you ever have to re-spray your Beetle, incidentally, it is worth considering using a 'stone-chip' paint on the vulnerable areas at the front of the car – the valance, luggage bay lid lower front end and the adjacent areas of the wings. Also, use stone chip on the lower front edges (the bottom six to eight inches) of the rear wings – these take a real battering from flying stones. Stone chip paints are thick and absorb energy from the missiles thrown up from the road surface, protecting the steel underneath. Don't – as I once was – be in too much of a hurry to topcoat stone chip paints, however, or the topcoat will be liable to cracking.

CREATURE COMFORTS

Not even the Beetle's most ardent admirer will pretend that the car offers much by way of luxury add-ons for the occupants. From the basic seating to the usually ineffectual heating and

Before launching into an interior customisation of your Beetle, do stop and reflect that the simple, minimalist standard interior (like the rest of the car) has a character and a charm all of its own.

windscreen de-misting, there are many areas in which the car can be improved.

Whether it is 'right' to make modifications to a Beetle is always going to be a fruitful source of disagreement between traditionalist and progressive owners, though. What to one person is a tastefully executed minor customisation can be anathema to another. Only you can decide whether modifying your own car would be an act of heresy or a 'radical chop' or 'Cal-look' triumph of aesthetics. Some Beetle owners

seem determined to match the wild looks of their cars with even wilder on-road performance; fine. If they get even half as much pleasure from their Bugs as I do from my stock 1500 then why not?

Perhaps reflecting the numbers of Beetle owners who like to customise their cars, the Beetle is considered fair game by the manufacturers of accessories – and it's always open season! There are probably more bolt-on goodies available for the Beetle than for any other car. The subjects of customisation and performance modification are vast and covered in specialised books; what follows is largely concerned with the process of making your Beetle

A beautiful show Baja from Bill Newton of Kentucky, which is as good a representation of the pinnacle of the customiser's art as I've seen. If you build a car which looks anything like as good as this, don't use it off-road! Show cars – whether stock or custom – are for show. (Photos Mike Key)

In Europe, the 'Cal' look usually involves pastel paintwork and ripping off all the chrome: but some Californians buck the trend. This is the interior of Dave Mason's 1962 bug, with all original dash (except the jumbo AutoMeter tachometer. It's the engine that's transformed in the Beetles owned by members, like Dave, of Der Kleiner Panzers.

a more enjoyable and comfortable car to drive, rather than cosmetics or 'How to make your Beetle out-drag a GTI on steroids'.

KEEPING WARM

The Beetle heating/demisting is always poor. Even on cars with sound heater channels and no unnecessary losses between the fan and heat exchangers, the heat exchangers and the windscreen outlet vents, there isn't enough heat to soften cream cheese, let alone melt ice or move condensation.

The great problem is that on a cold morning, the heater channels are stone-cold, and any warm air from the heat exchangers (which themselves take time to warm through) is chilled as it passes along the heater channels, so that it arrives at the screen at a temperature barely above freezing. It takes quite a few miles and a lot of air through the heater channels before the wall is warm enough to allow air to pass without chilling it.

One solution to the misted-up windscreen is an electric de-mister. These might typically output 120 Watts, which means a current requirement of 10 amps on a 12 volter – so don't turn it on and leave it running to demist the screen before you've started the engine and got some charge from the generator, because it would otherwise run the battery down alarmingly quickly. These useful accessories come with full fitting instructions – follow them to the letter, and try to find a heater which comes with an operating relay rather than having a switch in a 10 amp circuit.

Not so good at first-thing-in-the-morning screen demisting, but a definite overall improvement in heater efficiency, the recirculating air system draws air from the cab and passes this through the heat exchangers. Because the air in the cab warms up, the heat exchangers are re-heating pre-warmed air – much better than heating cold air drawn from outside the car.

The problem with the systems I've seen is

that you have to whip out the engine in order to cut a circular hole in the rear bulkhead. A 'Y' piece on the engine side connects to the heat exchanger pipes and a blower motor on the inside draws air from the cab – the engine's fan is not used. If you fit or have fitted a recirculating air system, remember that the fan must be running continuously – most especially during warmer weather – so that air is pushed through the heat exchangers; otherwise, the heat exchangers and with them the manifolds, would seriously overheat. This places a small constant drain on the battery which won't in itself cause any problems unless the battery is on the way out or not receiving a full charge from the generator.

There is one simple way to improve the effectiveness of the standard demister – open a quarterlight slightly! This draws air from the cab while the car is underway, and so helps suck more air in through the heat exchangers. Just thought I'd mention it.

KEEPING COOL

Speaking of ventilation, the Beetle's fixed rear and side windows don't allow a good throughflow of air but, happily, opening rear side window kits are available and not too difficult to fit. Hinged at the front ends, the windows really do suck lots of air out of the cab when the car's underway, so helping draw fresh air in through the door windows.

SUNROOF

Short of air conditioning, the ultimate in 'keepyou-cool' Beetle accessories is the sunroof. The Premier Division sunroof is the full-length folding 'Webasco' type, though many will settle instead for one of the modern translucent plastic jobs. In either case, fitting involves accurately cutting the roof (without distorting it) and the headlining, and it is usually best to buy from a company which will also fit the sunroof. The actual fitting charge will normally be the smallest part of the total price and, considering

Sunroof fitting. Cutting a great big hole in the roof of your Beetle is not a job for those of a nervous disposition. Possible glitches include discovering that your cutting line passes through the centre of a large dent filled to the brim with bodyfiller – some fairly skilled panel beating would be needed to sort that out. Go over the roof with a magnet, testing for filler, before deciding whether and exactly where to site a sunroof. Better still, leave it to a professional and, if you can afford it, have a new headlining fitted at the same time.

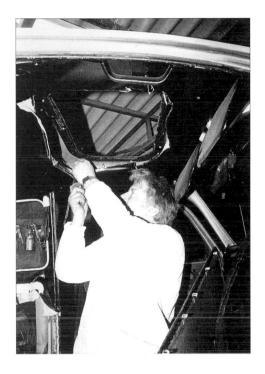

Fitting a headlining is, to say the very least, tricky. An experienced professional like Terry Ball can not only fit a headlining without ruining it – the results will look good for a long time.

My pal Em using my electric nibbler on his 1955 Ford Popular. These wonderful little tools (the nibbler, not the Pop) allow you to make ⅛" wide cuts in sheet steel with absolutely no distortion – which is vital for sunroof fitting. Equally importantly, they don't (like the angle grinder) leave razor-sharp edges! If you want to fit a sunroof, the nibbler is undoubtedly the best tool for cutting the roof.

that it is a sure-fire way to get a first class job, it is a small price to pay.

If you wish to fit your own sunroof, then I suggest investing in a nibbler; these devices fit into electric drills and 'nibble' a distortion-free ⅛" cut which – unlike angle grinders and air hacksaws – leaves edges which aren't as sharp as razors! Do take time to firstly go over where the cutting line will run in the roof inch by inch with a magnet to check for deep holes filled with bodyfiller or bridged with GRP – just in case the car has ever been rolled.

SEATS

Beetle seats never won awards for their comfort; those who suffer back problems will find these exacerbated by the total lack of lumbar support. I used to place a folded towel on the seat back to provide some padding for the small of my back (on blisteringly hot days, unfold the towel and drape it right down the seat back and base – keeps you cool), but there are more elegant solutions.

You want more comfortable seats? You cannot find a wider selection than that offered to Beetle owners. Sports seats, rally seats; seats so brightly coloured you should wear sunglasses before opening the door – you'll normally also have to fork out for a separate base and by the time you've bought matching rear seat covers and matching interior trim and carpets you can easily have spent more than the car originally cost. There is a far cheaper solution.

You can buy padded seat covers – these are usually available only in black or red and are intended primarily for boy racers to use in base model Golfs dressed up as GTIs. They generally have padding either side of the base – which stops you sliding from side to side on corners – and similarly either side of the back. It is a simple job to turn such a cover inside-out and, by trial and error, to add thin layers of foam padding until you have built up the right area sufficiently to give the necessary lumbar support.

How about some exclusivity? As an alternative to buying off-the-peg seats or covers, I commissioned a professional car upholsterer to make a set of 'bespoke' covers for one of my classics – leather faced, vinyl backed (the covers – not the upholsterer), and incorporating extra padding to give lumbar support – these covers transformed the seats from purgatory to 'favourite armchair' levels of comfort. The work took a couple of weeks and cost about the same as a pair of after-market ready-made covers.

INTERIOR TRIM

Before scrapping jaded trim and reaching for the chequebook to order a shiny new set, take time to try cleaning the trim, using a proprietary cleaning fluid and a toothbrush (which gets right into the surface grain). Then follow this up with a vinyl finishing liquid, available through motor factors. You may have a pleasant surprise and save a lot of money!

Tears in trim can be dealt with using various vinyl repair kits, but the wide availability and relatively low cost of repro Beetle trim encourage replacement rather than repair. If tears and scuff marks are not too prominent, however, it's worth reflecting that the state of the trim is actually in keeping with the vintage of the car; slightly down-at-heel trim can be more appropriate in a classic than too-shiny repro stuff – a point worth bearing in mind.

A full carpet set makes the cab feel cosier, but more importantly it cuts down road noise and in dampening the floorpans, cab noise. The brave can buy carpet on the roll, make paper templates, cut their carpet, edge stitch it so that it doesn't immediately begin to fray (an industrial sewing machine is necessary for this) and fit it. It's a lot easier to buy a tailored set of carpets, which should have the benefit of moulded heel panels to save on wear. With carpet, the secret is to buy the best quality you can afford – cheap carpets rarely last long.

Regularly vacuum cleaning the carpets

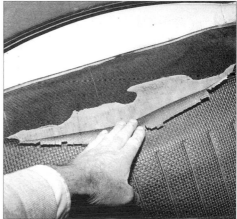

The rear seat back is a common casualty and, although vinyl repair kits are available, this one is too far gone.

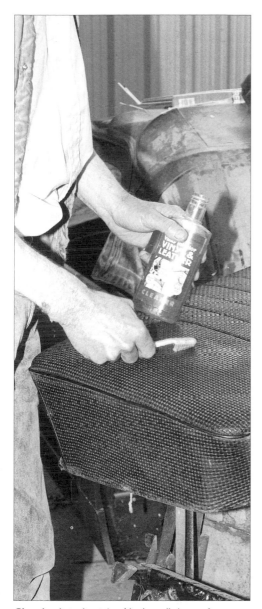

Cleaning interior trim. Vinyl usually has surface grain so, when you want to clean it, use an old tooth-brush to work the cleaner deep into the grain – if its not faded by long exposure to sunlight, it can come up like new.

lengthens their life by sucking out grit from your shoes which – if left to accumulate – acts as an abrasive. Fit underlay, and the sound-proofing qualities will be enhanced.

WINDSCREEN WASHERS

It's a pain having every week to check not only the level in the washer bottle but also the pres-sure in it or the spare tyre, and it is not difficult to fit an electric pump and bottle to replace the original set-up. You'll find washer bottles with integral (12 volt only) pumps at any motor accessory store; these should come with a line fuse and switch, plus full fitting instructions. Alternatively and at lower cost, you can salvage an electric pump and separate bottle from almost any car with the same polarity and volt-age as your Beetle, and fit one of these instead.

There is one compelling reason for modify-ing washer bottles which draw air from the spare tyre: if you suffer a flat tyre and fit the spare, the washers will be inoperative. Quite apart from the obvious dangers of driving a car with a dirty windscreen, a recent change in UK Police practice means that a Police Officer can deem a car unfit for use on the roads (instantly) if it fails any of around 200 criteria – including

Electric washer motor. A little windscreen washer motor – in this case, taken from an old Mini – can be discreetly hidden in the luggage bay. You'll also need some wire and a switch, a suitable bottle, a non-return foot valve and preferably a line valve to go in between the jets and the pump. The valves cost a couple of pounds each. I can foresee a time when bottles which rely on the spare wheel for their power are ruled illegal – if you have to fit the spare and put a deflated tyre in its place, you've no windscreen washers and – technically – the vehicle is unroadworthy. Better to fit a pressurised bottle. Better still, an electric pump.

working windscreen washers. If this happens, the car has to be towed off the road – it is an offence to move it on the public highway so much as an inch under its own power.

Swap the bottle for the self-contained, pre-charged variety – any Beetle specialist should be able to supply one of these off the shelf or, alternatively, salvage from a scrapped Beetle.

LIGHTS

Spot and fog lamps can make driving your Beetle safer; such units are widely available at motor factors and come with fitting instructions. The important point is that any extra lamps should not draw too high a current through existing wiring, yet at the same time, it is no bad thing to wire spot and fog lamps so that they can only be switched on when the existing system is live.

The solution is to take power direct from the battery (incorporate an in-line fuse if you do this) or from a spare connector on the fuse block, but to switch this circuit on and off by means of a relay – an electrically operated switch – which draws its meagre power need from the existing lighting circuit. Unless the lights are on, the relay won't operate and hence the extra lights cannot inadvertently be left switched on to drain the battery. Chapter four gives an introduction to auto electrics, but I recommend that extra lights are wired by an auto electrician.

Wire crimper in use. A crimping tool and a selection of terminals costs very little, and is very useful to have around. Purists will insist on soldering on terminals, which gives a bond rather than a mechanical joint. Unless you have experience of auto-electrics, I would always counsel leaving such work to an auto-electrician.

INSTRUMENTS

One of the most important gauges to be found on the dashboards of water-cooled cars is the coolant temperature gauge – if this starts to creep in the wrong direction then the aware driver can stop the car before any serious damage is done. The equivalent for the Beetle is the oil temperature gauge; oil, as we have already established, being the flat four's liquid coolant. There are two types of sender; one type fits in place of the dipstick, and the other in place of the drain plug. The former will show higher temperatures because the sender is higher up in the oil bath. If you intend to fit extra instrumentation, start with the oil temperature gauge.

OIL PRESSURE GAUGE

If you tend to push your Beetle hard then an oil pressure gauge is a very good insurance policy, because a small drop in pressure should precede any significant change in temperature (the warmer oil thins and the pressure drops slightly), giving you even more warning of impending engine damage.

VOLTMETER AND AMMETER

An a+mmeter measures all current flow to and from the battery save the 300 to 400 amp drain of the starter motor, and so it shows the state of charge or discharge. The problem with the ammeter is that thick wiring needed to carry sometimes quite heavy currents has to be run, with all the attendant risks. A voltmeter merely shows the rate of battery charge in volts – anything less than 13 volts indicates undercharging, much more than fourteen over-charging. Of the two, the voltmeter is arguably the more worthwhile.

It is, however, questionable whether the usefulness of either instrument warrants its cost – if a battery is slowly running low, you'll know because the starter motor will spin more slowly than usually; if the generator suddenly stops charging because the belt slips or breaks, the ignition light will come on.

TACHOMETER

Modern cars all benefit from the fitting of tachometers, but only because the engines are so quiet that they can slow and stall without giving you fair warning. In a Beetle, however, you are only too aware of what the engine revolutions are!

It is in motorsport that the tacho comes into its own. When you need to level the revs at, say, 3000 rpm before dropping the clutch in second gear for a quick getaway for a hillclimb or sprint, you'll be needing a tacho. In normal use, a tacho is nice to glance at occasionally, but hardly essential.

IN CAR ENTERTAINMENT (ICE)

In-car entertainment (ICE) equipment is a catch-all term nowadays applied to radios, cassette players, graphic equalisers and compact disc players.

Those with early cars might like to try and fit a basic period radio unit which is in keeping with the general character of their car. These units can be obtained from some specialists who have (showing great foresight) rescued many such radios over the years from scrapped cars, then serviced them and placed them into storage for future sale. These radios will not be cheap and you may in fact be asked to pay more than the price of a far better modern alternative. Most Beetle breakers and restorers will have a stock of period radios taken from scrapped cars, which gives you a cheaper alternative.

Modern ICE equipment is often very different from the equivalent which might have typically been fitted to a new Beetle. Not only has the range of types of equipment grown, but so have, in some instances, the dimensions. The radio aperture in a Beetle dashboard is too small to house some of today's more sophisticated ICE equipment.

It is possible to hang both the central ICE unit plus a graphic equaliser underneath the dashboard of the car, either using the standard

Meccano-like strips of metal which are provided for the purpose with most of this equipment, or by fitting a centre console. The drawback is theft. Thanks in large part to the quarterlight, Beetles are not especially difficult to break into (you can obtain after-market fittings which lock the quarterlight more securely). Theft of modern ICE equipment from parked cars is rife. If you are in two minds whether to fit a basic unit into the proper aperture or an expensive unit slung under the dash, bear in mind that thieves tend to steal only the better quality ICE equipment!

GENERAL INSTALLATION NOTES

Other electrical equipment in the car can cause interference and unwanted speaker noise when the car radio is in use. In general, you should try to keep components and leads – including the aerial lead – as far away from all elements of the ignition and direction indicator circuits as possible. Check that the unit has a good earth and the correct 1 amp or 2 amp in-line

fuse fitted. Also fit an in-line choke (available – as are other electrical components mentioned here – at motor factors or radio shops like Tandy) in the electrical supply to the radio, preferably as close as possible to the unit.

Using carbon rather than copper cored high tension leads removes one potential source of interference and is a more elegant solution than using resistive plug caps or in-line resistors in the HT leads.

The generator and contact breaker point ignition have the potential to cause interference; fit a .1 mf capacitor between an earth and the coil positive terminal, and another in between earth and the large terminal on the

Period radio. If you consider your Beetle a classic car then you will almost certainly want to fit a basic period radio and put up with fairly low quality mono output rather than modern equipment which sounds brilliant but still has to compete with the thumping of the boxer motor! People who salvage, repair and supply vintage car radios advertise in the classic car press.

generator. Electronic ignition systems have built-in suppression – don't fit a capacitor to the coil in this instance because you risk damaging the system if you do.

If, after taking the steps outlined here, interference is still a problem then there are specialist works available which may be able to help: alternatively, consult a specialist.

MANUAL CHOKE CONVERSION

Why fit a manual choke control? Surely automatic is better? Well, the problem with the Beetle choke is that it gives you about a minute of its time then switches off – in my case just as I reach the village and have to slow right down – so that you can find yourself having to keep blipping the throttle to keep the engine running if you hit slow or stationary traffic at the wrong time. The Beetle pedals are not especially suited to heel and toe-ing. If, on the other hand, your car has a manual choke, you can give it a bit of choke which not only enriches the mixture but also opens the throttle slightly, so that the engine ticks over a tad fast, but the even burble tells you the engine's basically happy and not about to die at the lights and embarrass you.

Those who live in the wide open spaces where stop-start motoring is unheard of probably won't benefit from a manual choke; if you live in town, it can be a real face-saver. Don't mess around with bits and pieces salvaged from other cars at a scrap yard though, just buy a kit.

FALSE ECONOMIES

Many gadgets claimed to reduce fuel consumption have been offered to the motorist over the years. At one time, it was possible to add up the percentage fuel savings claimed for the gadgets to over 100% so that, theoretically, if you fitted them all to your own car then it would run on fresh air!

The Trades Descriptions Act took care of some of the more ridiculous of these claims in the UK, but they did not do away with the fuel-saving gadget itself. It is not possible to state with 100% certainty that none of these devices can improve your fuel economy, but readers are generally advised to spend their money on having their cars' ignition and carburation systems correctly set up and maintained, rather than on fuel saving gadgetry. Remember that even if your ignition and carburation were perfectly set up, you could waste fuel if the car's tyre pressures were too low, or worse, if the rear brakes were binding.

Driving with binding brakes is rather like constantly driving up a very steep hill, and the fuel wastage is enormous. It is easy enough to test for binding brakes. Take the car for a short run (using the brakes a little to warm them up), then jack up one corner at a time and spin the wheels by hand. Binding will be obvious. The front disc brakes (where fitted) should drag very slightly when tested in this way, but if real rolling resistance is felt then remedial action will be necessary.

Rear drum brakes are adjustable, and slackening off the adjuster a fraction may or may not stop the binding. If not, the brake assembly will have to be stripped, freed and properly lubricated. If you have never undertaken this type of work before then either consult a good workshop manual before proceeding or have the work carried out professionally.

Binding of disc brakes is caused by sticking pistons within the callipers. Exchange calliper units are available, and offer the best option for the DIY enthusiast, although it is by no means impossible to service the callipers at home (consult a good workshop manual). Preferably, the work should be undertaken professionally.

Binding brakes can also be caused by problems with the master cylinder, or damaged brake lines – consult professionals if you have such problems.

Having too-low tyre pressures will not only increase fuel consumption, but it will also accelerate tyre wear. Do not be tempted to over-inflate the tyres to compensate, however, because this will also accelerate tyre wear, and more importantly it will reduce the road-holding of the car in certain circumstances. NEVER over-inflate Beetle front tyres. Whilst on the subject of tyres, the greatest cost saving you can make is not to get caught with illegal ones! In the UK, the fine *per illegal tyre* is enough to buy a complete new set of high quality tyres.

ECONOMY DRIVE

One of the greatest aids to fuel economy is a light accelerator foot! How you drive the car has a huge bearing on miles per gallon. If you go all out for speed between the bends and brake frequently, then you can expect maximum fuel consumption.

Driving economically, however, does not necessarily mean driving slowly. It takes a great amount of energy to accelerate a car to a fixed speed, and equally as much energy to stop it from that speed! Every time you apply the brakes, you are wasting energy (in the form of burnt mixture) which would otherwise help maintain your forward momentum. So the less you can use the brakes the better (this also saves on brake wear).

Reducing use of the brakes is easier and not as dangerous as it may at first sound. The secret is to do what any good driver should and to look and think ahead at all times. Instead of braking immediately before reaching a corner, try to slowly decelerate so that the car is travelling at the correct speed when you reach it, and treat obstacles in the road, such as parked vehicles which have to be passed, in the same way. Reducing acceleration and building up speed slowly instead can also save a lot of fuel, because cars drink petrol very quickly when the throttle is fully open. This may seem pretty obvious, but it is remarkable how many drivers seem not to understand that it is *rate of change* of speed, and not just speed, that swallows the gas. In both acceleration and braking, the accent is on driving the car as smoothly and gently as possible, consistent with road safety.

On long, straight roads, you can save fuel by reducing your speed to an optimum level consistent with available travelling time and road safety. Those who have driven cars with accurate fuel flow (MGP) meters on motorways will be aware that fuel consumption per mile travelled increases alarmingly along with speed. The exact speeds at which consumption increases will vary according to the type of car, but basically, remember that sixty miles per hour is cheaper than seventy, but more expensive than fifty-five! In the case of busy 'A' roads and motorways, however, the advantages of fuel saving are outweighed by the safety factor in keeping pace with traffic.

Many people are taking advantage of the cost savings offered by unleaded fuel in most countries today, and although unleaded fuel should NEVER be used in the standard Beetle, it is possible to use unleaded fuel in modified engines. These are now widely advertised and are available as exchange items. A substantial deposit, refundable on receipt of your old engine, may be levied. Before swapping engines in the interests of reducing pollution, reflect that unleaded fuel allegedly gives worse emissions than leaded unless it is used in conjunction with a catalytic converter. Worse, 'cats' only operate when they have reached a high operating temperature, so that a modern cat-equipped car burning unleaded fuel but used predominantly for short journeys might pump out far more pollution than a properly set-up Beetle burning leaded fuel. At the time of writing, no known after-market catalytic converter is available for the Boxermotor – nor is any likely to be made available, unless legislation forces it. Bearing in mind that pollution is a global problem, it is not inconceivable that catalytic converters will become mandatory on new cars in Mexico or Brazil; should this happen, cat exhaust systems for Beetles would probably be shipped to Europe.

CHAPTER THREE

Surviving Restorers and Restoration

Whether DIY or professional, we are talking cutting-edge survival here, and a lot of people don't last the course, running out of motivation, money or commonly both and ending up with a part-restored and unusable car, plus a gaping hole in the bank balance. Don't believe me?, then check out all of those part-restored cars which you see advertised for sale. In each and every case, the would-be restorer has got out of his or her depth, will normally already have spent far more money on the restoration than the car is worth in its half-completed state, and will usually have to take a depressing loss on the sale. The decision to cut losses and sell a part-restored car is not one which is ever taken lightly, and behind every such 'distress' sale lies a story of abject misery.

Restoration involves taking what is effectively a dead or dying Beetle and bringing it back to full health – in the process, spending a lot of money and time (DIY restoration) or one heck of a lot of money (professional restoration) on it. Exactly how much time and/or money a full Beetle restoration actually involves will probably come as a surprise to anyone who has never completed a restoration.

A full DIY restoration (which incorporates a bodyshell-off chassis rebuild, the majority of mechanical and electrical components being repaired and painted or renewed) might typically take a thousand hours and upwards of your time – that's the equivalent of six months' worth of forty hour weeks. A good professional Beetle specialist restoration company might be able to complete the bodywork restoration in perhaps four weeks (if you undertake some of the initial stripdown, the rebuild, the paint preparation and painting yourself) to six weeks – 160 to 240 hours,

which will be costed at so much per hour. At the time of writing, a UK restoration workshop rate of ten pounds an hour would be considered very low, and the labour charge alone for the restoration would therefore be from £1,600 upwards – plus painting. The reasons why a professional workshop can restore a Beetle so much more quickly than the amateur, incidentally, are several. The professional has the tools and equipment to speed work which the amateur must painstakingly complete by hand; the amateur will spend countless hours salvaging components and trim which the restorer will replace in minutes as a matter of course; either with a brand-new item bought at trade price or very often with a part in better condition salvaged from one of the scrap cars which most Beetle restorers keep on their premises for the purpose.

Sticking with 1994 prices, the average parts and labour charges for a quality full professional restoration appear to be in the region of £5,000 to £6,000. That 'ball park' figure applies to an MOT failure car which is transformed into what can best be described as a 'new, second-hand car'. For that sort of money, you could expect the bodywork to be completely sound and rust-free, the mechanical components to be either reconditioned or replaced with new. Such a car should last as long as a brand-new 1994 car and, seen in that light, five grand seems a small price to pay.

Of course, the time and money requirement for a restoration is entirely dependent on the standards you strive for (or are willing to accept). Many 'restored' Beetles – both from cowboy professionals and amateurs – are actually 'bodged' Beetles! The Beetle itself is no better nor worse than any other classic in this respect, and the reasons why most classic cars

Whether your car is restored at home on a DIY basis or by professionals, there are a host of pitfalls which can make survival a formidable challenge.

are bodged are that their DIY 'restorers' don't have enough of the folding stuff to do the job correctly, that they don't possess the facilities, skills or motivation to do the work properly, and consequently they start taking short cuts or – if they have the work carried out by a cowboy – that they lack the money to have the work carried out to a good standard. In the case of the amateur, rather than shell out on a new door skin which they would probably make a hash of fitting anyway, they plaster GRP and bodyfiller over rotten holes in the existing skin. Rather than cut out and replace

structural steel, they bridge holes with cardboard or rolled-up newspaper covered with bodyfiller, chicken wire, concrete and even papier mâché – I've seen it all, and the really sad part is that the most skilled bodgers can make the cars they butcher look really good.

Somewhere in between the expensive 'new, second-hand Beetle' and the cheap completely bodged nail, you'll find the majority of restored cars. Rotten steel will have been cut out and replaced with sound (although expect to find some evidence of 'MOT' welded repairs – cover patches – on most Beetles), the engine will be a reconditioned unit capable of lasting many years without major overhaul. The interior might be a bit tatty and showing its age, the majority of the original mechanical and electrical components might have been cleaned, repaired and painted rather than replaced, the paintwork might not have a mirror finish. The result is a reasonably smart and usable car at a price which does not entail taking out a mortgage.

SURVIVING DIY RESTORATION

Relatively few people actually carry out full amateur restorations, although plenty of people claim to have done so, even in cases where the bulk of the work was carried out by professionals. Restoration is, you see, widely regarded as something macho, an achievement which raises the prestige of the 'restorer' and the esteem in which they are held by their fellow enthusiasts. In fact, once you realise the sort of work a typical DIY restoration entails, you'll see that there is little, technically, to boast of.

Only those who have tried restoration will know what's involved; people whose knowledge is based on what they have read actually know nothing. This is because most written works on the subject describe restorations carried out by professionals who, naturally, fail to inform the writers of their occasional disasters (every restorer has disasters, though no professional is ever going to admit to the fact!) or of the short-cuts and questionable practices they might occasionally resort to. Some pundits who talk or write authoritatively about restoration might in fact have no substantial first-hand experience of the subject. They describe restoration in almost fairy-tale fashion – a magical world where nothing ever goes wrong, no-one ever gets injured and everyone lives happily ever after.

Read an account of a restoration and you'll read of intrepid cutting and welding, heroic panel beating and epic spannering – all of which are part and parcel of restoration but nevertheless only a small part of the process. The bulk of work in any amateur restoration is in fact cleaning; scraping off old underseal and chipping or flatting away old bodyfiller, linishing away or wire brushing off surface rust, stripping paint, cleaning accumulated grease and dirt from suspension components – paint preparation alone can take weeks of part-time work – not macho, not highly skilled work, but mind-numbingly boring tedium – something not to brag about but to grudgingly admit to only when pressed.

The tedious nature of much of the work of restoration is one of the factors which can sorely test your motivation – it's difficult to summon up any enthusiasm, for instance, for leaving a cosy house in mid-winter in order to freeze your joddler off in the workshop doing some mundane cleaning or scraping.

Another hazard to motivation is that things can – and often do – go wrong. When freshly applied paint blooms, blisters, runs, sags or cracks, when a line of spot welds springs open or you blast through a repair panel with the Mig, when you wreck a component whilst struggling to undo the hopelessly seized nut and bolt which secure it – it is difficult to avoid going into deep depression and terminating the restoration.

The solution to nearly all restoration disasters is to Walk Away And Leave It. Lock up the workshop if necessary, because if you keep on working when your mood has blackened then you will only succeed normally in making matters worse. Forget all about restoration and do something completely different, something which puts you in a good frame of mind. Whatever problems you encounter, even those which seem insurmountable, all seem somehow less traumatic the following day.

DIY restoration offers enormous potential to injure yourself. Razor-sharp edges on panels demand that you wear stout leather gauntlets, but you'll find that it is near-impossible to work with them on and so most people take their chances with the steel and keep a box of sticking plasters handy (blood appears to accelerate rusting of steel, so as soon as you've

Restoration isn't all about welding, panel beating and paint spraying. Most of the time is spent cleaning and scraping. Old underseal can hide all sorts of nasties – best to scrape it off and take a look underneath.

Freshly-painted Beetle. Nothing looks lovelier than a classic car wearing a fresh coat of paint; unfortunately, this is true even of bodged Beetles which, within a year or two, will see rust staining erupting through the surface of the paint. With restoration – get it right first time rather than cut corners and have to re-do the lot in a year or two.

Expect to find anything from welded-on cover patches to papier mâché here; look from the inside of the car, under the rear seat. Hidden from view – anything goes!

attended to first-aid, remember to wipe the offending panel clean). Spanners fly off rounded nuts and you hand smashes into hard, sometimes sharp and unyielding objects, molten globules from your Mig welder fall down the inside of your shoe and burn their way into your foot (note: THIS HURTS!), paint stripper quickly dispenses with the outer layers of your skin and gnaws at the nerve endings underneath. DIY restoration can be hell.

Not everyone is really suited to DIY restoration – it takes a particular type of mentality to see the job through (you don't have to be crazy to restore a car, but if you are, it undoubtedly helps!). For a start, you have to relish hard work – lots of it. Despite the wide availability of modern labour-saving powered tools, there are still plenty of jobs for which there is no substitute for a hand tool and elbow grease. Secondly, you have to be strong willed enough to shrug your shoulders and get on with the job when things go – sometimes disastrously – wrong. If the final over-thinned topcoat reacts with an underlying and incompatible coat then you might have to strip the lot back to bare metal and start all over again – wasting weeks of preparation and scrapping perhaps a hundred pounds' worth of paint. You need almost blind optimism in order to be able to fool

yourself that, no matter how bad things look at present, they are going to get better. At the same time, you have to retain a degree of pessimism, so that setbacks – when they occur – don't surprise and depress you.

The ideal DIY restorer is the mule-headed, masochistic pessimist who yet knows that things can eventually come right.

Your entire approach to restoration can make life easier or harder – it's up to you. I find that decorating the workshop with nice prints of finished Beetles can prove just the incentive to keep going when I'm exhausted and might otherwise pack in for the day. Put a heater and a chair in the workshop, so that you have somewhere warm and comfortable to sit when the time comes to stop working and think things out – so much better than retiring to the house from where, once you've sunk into your favourite armchair, you probably won't re-emerge that day.

A workshop without a radio is a cold, unwelcoming place – install one and tune in to a station which broadcasts relaxing music. Perhaps fittingly, classical music is ideal for me, and chat shows are deadly – I find myself being drawn into the arguments and getting into a temper and thus making unnecessary mistakes for no good reason.

Try to become more organised. Build a tool board so that all your important tools are constantly to hand, build more storage for the myriad of fittings which will have to come off the car and maintain a list of spares which you are going to need so that these can be ordered in time and you don't end up wasting time whilst urgently needed spares are in the post.

TOOLS AND FACILITIES

Before you launch headlong into a restoration, you'll need to acquire somewhere to work and the tools to do the job. It is by no means impossible to carry out a restoration in the open; nor is it impossible to dig your garden using a teaspoon – neither are recommended. The workshop should ideally be high enough to house a Type 2 and large enough to hold two cars, so that you have sufficient height to be able to lift the bodyshell from the chassis and somewhere dry to keep the two until they are reunited. You'll also need space for a workbench, tools and spares storage. It should be dry, relatively draught-free (although some circulation of air is no bad thing) and, above all, it must have a sound concrete floor, able to withstand heavy loads concentrated into small foot prints – i.e., the weight of the car when supported by a jack or axle stands.

To build a suitable structure from scratch can cost as much as a good quality restoration – and that's before tools are taken into consideration. In addition to a good set of general mechanic's tools, a range of specialised tools for cutting, cleaning and welding bodywork will usually be acquired.

Even if you bring in an outside welder to do the actual welded repair, a Mig welder with which you can tack panels into position in preparation is a 'must'. Then you need an air compressor – not only for paint spraying but also to power air tools if your budget runs to them, and also to blow out minor welding fires and to blow dust out of nooks and crannies prior to painting.

DIY Mig. This is my own Mig welder. It's gasless and uses cored wire which is expensive – but at least you only have one consumable to run out of. Some of the Migs which have been offered to the DIY market during the 1980s have been of very poor build quality, but happily this seems nowadays to be a thing of the past. Consequently, I would always advise anyone seeking a DIY Mig to buy new.

In reality, much of the vast range of specialist tools offered to the restorer nowadays is superfluous – in most instances, there are alternative – cheaper – tools which can do, or can be adapted to do, the same job as more expensive tools. For example, you could buy in a wide range of steel cutting tools for cutting out rotten steel; a nibbler, angle grinder, air hacksaw, air chisel and so on, but a hacksaw and padsaw can usually give exactly the same results – albeit more slowly!

Good quality tools are preferable to the cheap stuff, because cheap tools usually break just as you really need them – and when tools break they often damage the components or fittings on which they are being used. However, good quality tools (apart from those which fall off the backs of lorries) are for many, prohibitively expensive. If so, buy cheap sets of spanners, screwdrivers etc. initially, but replace those which wear out (which obviously receive the highest use) with better quality alternatives. If you do this, you'll probably find that the 11, 12, 13 and 14mm spanners get the highest usage and hence wear out first. The same applies to sockets. It is always cheaper to buy tools in sets rather than, for instance, to buy individual sockets and slowly build up a set.

Buy the best in components and consumables. For example, you can find reconditioned exchange gearboxes and engines offered by back-street companies at very low prices, but it is always better to buy from a recognised specialist supplier and to pay the higher price which they will charge. It is far from unknown for some cheap 'reconditioned' engines to turn out on inspection to have merely been cleaned and painted!

Similarly, it is generally better to shell out and buy quality repair panels and especially fittings such as bumpers, running boards and the like, than to buy cheap ones and have to replace them a couple of years on when the chrome has all but disappeared. Cheap paint and thinners will not only jeopardise the paint finish, but will usually be more difficult to work with than good quality stuff.

RECONSTRUCTION VS RENOVATION

The term 'restoration' is widely used to describe two separate processes; reconstruction and renovation. For a car like the Beetle for which almost all spares from a bodyshell to a bolt can be bought, new, off the shelf, it is tempting to renew the majority of components during a restoration rather than strip, clean, repair, rebuild and paint – in other words, renovate – them. Reconstruction saves time but costs money; renovation saves money but can take years.

The cause of most financially-challenged unfinished restorations is too great an emphasis on reconstruction; the hapless 'restorer' buys loads of goodies as and when needed or when the mood takes him, rather than firstly establishing a budget and working out exactly which components can be renewed and which will have to be salvaged.

Most restorations are a mix of reconstruction and renovation; components which are fairly easily salvaged are cleaned, repaired and repainted, other, more complex components – the engine being the most obvious, or the transaxle – might be replaced or swapped for professionally reconditioned units. The more components you are able to salvage, the cheaper the restoration will be. Perhaps the worst trap to fall into is to salvage tired mechanical and electrical components which should really be replaced, and to spend the money saved on shiny bumpers, new interior trim and so on. Many people fall into this trap, as the large number of superb-looking but unreliable classic cars on the roads proves.

THE RESTORATION

And so to the restoration itself. Not every restoration is a full restoration, and many people tackle the various jobs in isolation when money and time permit, keeping the car on the road in between times. This is generally known as a 'rolling' restoration, and its advantages are that you retain nearly full use of the car throughout (save the occasional few days when major jobs are attended to) and that the work proceeds according to available time and finance. The drawbacks to a rolling restoration are firstly that it is never complete; by the time you think you've finished, the first areas you worked on usually require re-doing, and secondly, because not every component receives attention as it would in a full restoration, you can expect intermittent component failures when you drive the car.

Many people who restore their Beetles avoid – to save work – separating the bodyshell and chassis: this is a big mistake. They weld in new floor edge repair panels from underneath the car ('upside-down' welding is difficult, quite dangerous and inevitably unsightly). They then hack out the old heater channels, force the floorpan edges downwards and hammer in the replacement heater channels before welding these up. But wait a minute? Where's the belly pan gasket? You guessed it – either there ain't one or it's cobbled up from short lengths of gasket worked into position – either way, water is going to find its way in and the new heater channels/floorpan edges won't last long.

A proper, full restoration comprises several separate stages: the stripdown, chassis/engine/running gear repair, welding in new floorpans or floorpan repair sections, bolting new heater channels onto the floorpan edges, cutting the old heater channels from the shell then reuniting the body and chassis and welding the heater channels to the body, lifting the body complete with new heater channels back off so that a belly pan gasket can be fixed into position, reuniting the body and chassis for the last time, followed by sundry bodywork welded repair and, finally, building the car back up. Sounds easy if you say it fast.

STRIPDOWN

Despite horrors such as hopelessly seized or rounded nuts and bolts and the physical strain involved in removing the engine (and especially the transaxle) and lifting the bodyshell from the chassis, it is relatively easy to take a Beetle to pieces. Fools rush (headlong) into this part of the restoration whereas smart people firstly photograph every part of the car so that they know what components came from where (your workshop manual might not be too useful in this respect; even if there is a photograph of an area it will often prove to be of a different year of car with different fittings etc.), then take the time and trouble carefully to sort and store components so that **a)** they can be found when the time comes to rebuild the car, **b)** those components are sorted according to whether they can be re-used with no attention, whether they need renovating or whether they are shot and will have to be replaced and **c)** so that they don't get eaten by mice, don't rust away or get trodden on by workshop visitors.

Two experienced people could easily rip a Beetle down to a rolling chassis in a day. The first-time novice restorer, working slowly and methodically, should allow many times as long. Make notes and take photographs as you go along so that you don't end up rebuilding the engine tinware before you have fitted the inlet manifold or spending hours trying to figure out what component that captive nut on the engine bay side wall is supposed to hold (as already mentioned, the Beetle has been subjected to in excess of 80,000 production modifications – don't be surprised if a captive nut turns out to be superfluous for your own car).

Your normally invaluable workshop manual might be found wanting when you are stripping a car for restoration: Most workshop manuals are based on work carried out on a new or nearly-new example of the Beetle rather than a rotten old restoration project car and probably won't even mention what do to when a wing or rear body mounting bolt head refuses to budge, shears clean off or when its 'captive' nut breaks free. The secret of dealing with obstinate nuts, bolts and screws is to try penetrating oil, when that fails, to apply heat to expand the female part of the fastening (when it is safe, of course, don't use a blowtorch anywhere near fuel or brake hydraulic components) and, if that fails, to cut or grind it off. Most people, following their workshop manual instructions, simply attack the fitting and, when it refuses to move, apply more and more force to it until something gives. Quite apart from the personal injury you risk when a nut rounds, the spanner flies off and your hand smashes into something inevitably sharp, the component which is held by the fitting can also become damaged and might be ruined. Worse, parts of the bodywork can become distorted.

The first job is to disconnect (earth strap first) and remove the battery. There is now no chance of a spanner shorting some live terminal to earth. Next, drain then remove the fuel tank, *and store it in another building*. Then, bleed the braking system dry. You have just removed

What fits here? Does anything fit here? The Beetle, more than most cars, had so many production modifications that superfluous captive nuts, holes etc. are commonplace. If you have 'before' photos to look at, you'll see exactly what, if anything, the nut/hole is there for. The purpose of this hole in the engine bay lid is a typical example!

Battery disconnection. The first step in almost any repair is to disconnect the battery so that electrical fires cannot occur. Disconnect the earth first – then the live terminal. If you disconnect the live terminal first and your spanner touches any earthed metal part of the car, you will short out the battery –so be warned.

Window removal. If the rubber is perished and you intend to replace it, cut away the outer lip with a craft knife and the windows will come out easily. Otherwise, it's a matter of one person inside the car pushing with his or her feet, and another outside ready to catch the screen.

Be careful when lifting out the glass, especially when working on your own – leather gloves would be a good precaution.

Take care when removing the old seal so that you don't accidentally kink the chrome trim. It would prove nigh-on impossible to re-fit damaged trim.

Stripping the door furniture is not too difficult (with the exception of the winder mechanism), and worth the hassle for a decent respray.

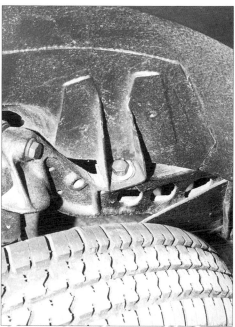

Rear body mounting nuts. Use a hexagonal 17mm socket to get these turning – a twelve pointer can simply round them. You'll have to clean approximately half a ton of dirt out of the bracket before to you even see these bolts.

the main causes and fuel sources of terminal fires and – it must be said – explosions.

I believe in removing more fragile components before they get damaged in the rough and tumble of restoration, so I would then remove all salvageable soft trim – seats, door and side panels, carpets and mats, and store it in the house, where it is dry and safe from rodent attack. Then the glass comes out – windows, lights and mirrors and, for a bare metal re-spray, the instruments.

Those whose Beetles have MacPherson strut front ends will do well to make up some kind of trolley to support the frame head and allow the chassis to be wheeled around once the bodyshell is off. Do take steps to strengthen the bodyshell before lifting it from the chassis – steel rods welded across the door apertures and side to side cross braces (one between the two A posts, another between the B posts and X-braces to keep the lot rigid) can prevent distortion. The bolts which hold the heater channels to the floorpan are usually very obstinate

but, because the heater channels (and with them the captive nuts) are inevitably to be replaced, it does not matter if they shear. The two 17mm headed rear body mounting bolts are another matter – use heat to expand the casting into which they run – shear these and you will certainly make a lot of unnecessary work for yourself!

To minimise the risk of injury to people or damage to the car, use four sturdy supports of around three feet in height – two either side of the car – with steel bars placed on top to support the shell. Lift one end of the shell, slide across the steel bar, then raise the other end and support that. The chassis can then be rolled out from underneath and the bodyshell lowered ready for welded repair. If you leave

This is the relatively painless way of manoeuvring the Beetle bodyshell when off the chassis. The bodyshell is balanced on a small trolley fitted with robust castors.

the engine and transaxle in situ whilst the bodyshell is removed, you'll find both much easier to get at.

BODYWORK

Until you've actually stripped the car down, you cannot with 100% certainty adjudge the condition of the bodywork, and it can be taken as a general rule that the bodyshell turns out to be in a far worse state than you could possibly have imagined. When the flitch panel turns out to resemble a patchwork quilt or to be so thoroughly rotten that nothing short of complete replacement will do, when the edges of the adjoining panels turn out to be thoroughly rotten as well, only the strongest-willed will be able to summon the strength to keep going.

If a major panel such as a flitch or full quarter panel needs replacing, it is worth considering handing this specific job over to a

Don't automatically assume that you've no option other than to buy in new panels to replace rotten ones, it is possible to salvage even large panels like this flitch from scrapped cars at far lower cost.

professional. It won't take an experienced restorer very long to do just the one job in isolation (and should not, therefore, cost too much) and you should – in theory – end up with a straight bodyshell.

This book is all about survival, but it is in fact better to accept that a bodyshell is beyond economic repair and to seek out a car in better condition, than it is to put on a pair of blinkers and soldier hopelessly on, yet many people take the latter course. In some cases, it is better to mutter "Ah well, these things are sent to try us" – or words to that effect – and terminate the restoration.

WELDED REPAIRS

The majority of Beetles – along with the majority of lowish-value classics – go through the 'jalopy' stage before anyone regards them as classic cars. By this I mean that they reach a stage of decay at which they start to need sundry welded repairs in order to make it through the annual MOT test. Short of non-ferrous (GRP, cement etc) bodging, 'MOT welding' is the basest form of bodywork repair. It is normally done to the very minimum standards needed to get an MOT certificate for

If anyone ever attempts to convince you that Mig welding is easy, they're either telling fibs, an armchair expert with no first-hand experience – or both. When you have learned how not to blast holes in expensive repair panels, when you are impervious to the pain of molten globules of weld burning into your skin, when you are an experienced fire-fighter, then you'll be able to call yourself a Mig welder, my son. The mask and gauntlets are essential when Mig welding – the extra clothing helps protect you from molten globules of weld. Welding on a hot summer's day is not a pleasant experience, but good if you wish to lose some weight!

another year, and the repairs often don't last for the whole year!

MOT welding almost invariably consists of slapping a cover patch over the area of rotten steel. Because the rot is not cut out, it continues to spread underneath the patch, which itself usually rots along its welded edges due to welding residue which attacks the thin steel. Twelve months later, the car again fails – or threatens to fail – the MOT and a larger patch is welded on top of the original – again, curing nothing and actually accelerating future rusting by creating a nice enclosed area for the rot to develop in. This process can go on for years, and I have seen a Beetle flitch panel sporting seven layers of patches!

MOT standards are constantly extended, and one day they might even put a stop to MOT welded repairs. That will be all for the good, because it's far more difficult to put right an MOT bodge than it is to deal with honest bodyrot.

It is possible to deal with a panel which has an area of rot – without resorting to the cover patch – by butt welding. The process is simple. First, the area of rot is cut out, so that there is strong and clean steel to weld to. Then a paper or cardboard template is cut and, from this, you cut out a steel repair patch which is a snug fit in the hole. This takes time but, if there are no gaps between the repair panel edges and the edges of the hole, the chances of burning through with the Mig and making yet more work for yourself are greatly reduced. Clean the edges to be welded back to bare metal, put masking tape on the edges and paint the rest of the repair panel, then spray weld-through zinc paint onto the edges. Tack this into position and, when it is securely held, seam weld it. Finally, clean and paint the repair and surrounding steel. Because there is no overlapping steel, there are no enclosed areas to rot and, provided that all weld residue is cleaned off before the paint is applied, the repair will last as long as the rest of the car!

Butt welding thin section steel demands great care to avoid burning through, and an easier alternative is to make the repair patch very slightly oversize and to place a stepped edge all around so that, when fitted, the stepped edge just overlaps the edges of the existing steel.

The next step up from a butt welded repair patch is the proprietary repair panel – door skin lower edges, quarter panel lower sections, and so on. These can vary in quality and most especially in fit from excellent to abysmal – the worst won't fit unless you are prepared to spend a lot of time re-shaping them! Repair panels are normally dipped in a black paint to protect them from rust – clean this off and you may discover areas of established rusting as well as areas of contamination where the paint does not adhere and, for this reason, it is good practice to clean all the paint off and apply your own before welding the panel in. Treat the edges to be welded to a coating of zinc-based weldable primer and the panel should last forever. Use a 40 grit disc to clean off the old paint; this stuff doesn't succumb to stripper, and the scoring made by an abrasive disc gives your own paint something to get a good strong grip on.

Of course, it is always better to cut out a part-rotted panel completely, and to weld in a full replacement panel. In some instances, this allows you to use a spot welder rather than Mig or gas – spot welds are strong and far and away the neatest repair method. If you can use a spot welder then count how many original welds there were on any seam, and use the same number of welds when you come to re-weld it. If the original welds were at half inch intervals, for instance, then make your own welds at the same frequency to maintain the original strength.

Most amateur and professional restorers use Mig welders on any areas they cannot use the spot welder. Mig welding is anything but easy – and if anyone tries to tell you otherwise – they're nothing more than an armchair expert!

For a start, it can be difficult to even see what you are welding, and it's all too easy to drift away from the actual joint and set a course across the panel instead – keep checking as you go. Secondly, the Mig settings, the wire feed speed and the speed of the gun across the steel must be spot-on – otherwise, you'll blow a hole in the panel or fail to get proper penetration

Stepped edge repair – stepping the edge. Placing a step in the edge of a panel allows you to use self-tapping screws or pop rivets to draw them tightly together, aligning them in the process. The technique is most commonly used on quarter panel repairs, where it is essential that the old and new metal lie flush.

Stepped edge repair – edge stepping tools. I made an edge-step tool (these are also called joddlers, jogglers, jodders etc.) by welding two hand-filed blocks into an old self-locking (Mole) wrench. The one on the right is bought in, and incorporates a punch for making holes for 'plug' welding.

As this shot shows, one of the biggest problems with MiG welding is seeing what is happening at the sharp end!

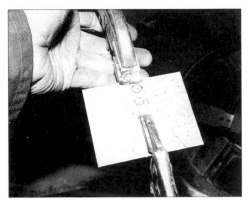

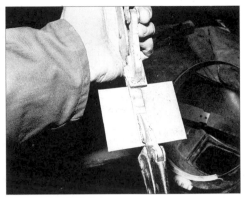

Stepped edge repair – plug welding. Plug welds replicate spot welds, and offer a quick and easy welded repair method. Seam welding is more difficult, and needs a lot of practice.

Seen from the back, the weld has penetrated fully, and the joint will be very strong.

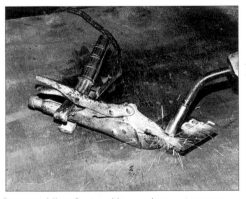

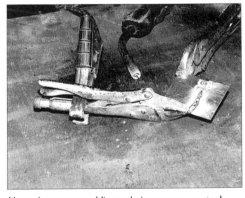

Seam welding. Seam welding produces a very strong joint, but is more difficult to achieve than plug welding, and there's inevitably a lot more proud weld to be ground away afterwards.

Always hone your welding techniques on scrap steel, and don't weld up the bodyshell until you've mastered the basics. After taking this photograph, I bent the join to see whether the plug or the seam weld was stronger – if anything, the plug weld was.

and have a weak joint as a result. Thirdly, any contamination – rust, paint, greases – on the surface or underside of the steel can result in a weak joint. Last and by no means least, the heat build-up created by welding causes panels to expand, so that two flush panels can suddenly spring apart and you burn one edge away rather than join the two together. In extreme cases, the heat build-up can corrugate the panel.

Then there's the fire hazard. Sparks from a Mig welder (not to mention globules of molten weld) are quite capable of setting any flammable material on fire. This includes sound-deadening materials and trim on the inside of the

Floorpan replacement. Drill out the floorpan edge spot welds and part the seams – grind out the corners.

First floorpan welded in, heater channel bolted on (right). This is the first real milestone in the restoration.

A comparatively rare sight – a Beetle with 100% sound floopans and heater channels!

Meanwhile, the bodyshell – internally braced – awaits with understandable trepidation having its old heater channels cut out.

car, plus the many and varied highly combustible materials to be found in the restoration workshop.

Sometimes, materials which you would not think of as especially dangerous in this respect turn out to be the worst – wire wool, for instance, burns with a ferocity which will amaze, and brake fluid is more combustible than petrol.

As you cut and weld, you need to constantly check that everything is still in correct alignment – it is far from unusual for a restorer who is paint prepping a Beetle to suddenly notice that the entire front-end is skewed... This

The heater channels are removed with the aid of an air hacksaw, chisel etc.

Quarter panel repair. Don't fit the entire repair pressing as supplied if you can cut it down and still find strong steel to weld it to – that way, when it rusts out again, you can still use the small repair panel rather than a full quarter panel.

means taking endless measurements and checking levels with a spirit level, welding in temporary braces to assist in the accurate positioning of repair and replacement panels. Even better, offer up adjacent panels, wings, doors to ensure that lines are correct before welding in anything. This quite naturally slows you up – don't rush.

For all welded repairs, the process which takes the least time is the actual welding. You can spend hours, days or even weeks, cutting out the rot, fabricating and prepping the repair panel and the area around the repair – and weld it up in a few minutes. Most armchair experts on restoration can talk only of cutting and welding, their lack of first-hand experience means that they just don't know how little time is spent in these activities, and how much on preparation. Because it takes such a short time to do the actual welding, there is a strong case for bringing in professionals to do this.

A professional welder is a hundred times better than even the most talented amateur – simply because the professional has such vast experience of welding. A really good weld needs little if any grinding-down afterwards – most amateur attempts look like an incontinent pigeon has wandered along the join. The good weld will achieve full penetration and be far stronger than the usual amateur effort.

Because mobile welders charge by the hour, the costs of bringing one in to weld up, say, heater channels, perhaps A and B post bottoms and a quarter panel repair panel won't be very high as long as you can prepare enough work to keep the professional occupied for an hour or two per visit. Most professional welders are also quite talented tin-bashers, and will be able to perform any necessary re-shaping of repair panels before they are welded in.

PAINTING AND PAINT PREPARATION

I hope that by now you are getting an idea of what DIY car restoration is actually like – the

Before you start on the paintwork, decide exactly how much work you can handle – painting the interior, for instance, means stripping the lot out. Try cutting the existing paint – it might come up well, and save a lot of work.

pain, the slog, the anguish. Well – just to cheer you up – the single facet of restoration with the greatest potential for things to go expensively wrong, and the hardest grind in the entire restoration process, concerns paintwork.

Automotive paintwork is too vast a subject to be covered comprehensively in a book such as this, and there are some excellent works which go into great detail – notably, *Vehicle Refinishing* by Pat North, (Osprey Automotive).

Just as in welding, the time needed to spray a coat of paint is the merest fraction of what it takes to prepare the bodyshell for the spraying. The first question to be addressed is whether

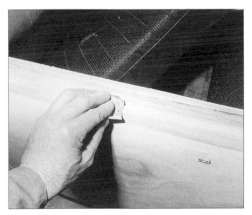

Pay attention to small details, and never rush paint preparation. Here, I'm flatting the existing paintwork that normally lives under the side window rubber.

Rust on the nearside door. I flatted the surface rust away, then brush-painted on a rust-resistant paint ready for priming. Leave even the tiniest trace of rust under your paintwork and you will find russet staining on the paint within a year.

Wire under window rubber for respray. If you want that 'bare metal' respray look but don't want all the hassle of removing all the windows, work a length of insulated wire under the screen rubbers' lips so that the paint is able to flow underneath. It is advisable, however, to remove the screens altogether. Not only does this ensure that the aperture lips are painted, but it also gives you a chance to deal with any rusting of said lip.

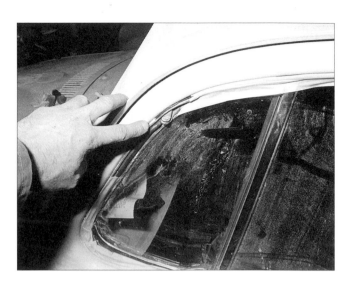

to remove the existing paint completely and take the shell back to bare steel (which entails a complete stripdown – which can take months), or whether to simply flat the paint and spray more on top.

The great problem with flatting and overcoating the existing paint is the fact that you don't know exactly what lies under that paint, and many substances which could be there might react adversely with the paint you choose to work with. Tiny traces of polish nestling in surface scratches will react; aerosol tin blow-in paint repairs with an unsuitable paint can react. I sprayed a Beetle roof panel in high-build cellulose primer, and found several small areas of reaction, where the cellulose thinners softened and penetrated the outer surface of the existing paint, found something it didn't like underneath and proceeded to attack it. The result was blistering.

I took some of these areas back to bright steel, and still the cellulose reacted! In this instance, something was actually in the surface of the steel itself, and only after a lot of cleaning and de-greasing was I able to paint the offending steel.

There is an easier way to deal with paint

reaction, and that is to spray on a barrier coat – a paint which is not affected by cellulose thinners. I'm not especially proud of using these paints, but in the past they have got me out of trouble many times. Your local trade automotive paint supplier will be able to supply you with a barrier coat if needed.

Whilst writing this book I was respraying my own Beetle. Knowing from past experience that there is one layer of paint on the shell which reacts with cellulose, I elected to wet flat the entire shell, apply a coat of barrier coat, then proceed with primer and topcoats. The barrier coat itself had a very thick sediment at the bottom of the tin which I spent ages stirring back into suspension, after which, the paint seemed to be too thick. After spraying the shell, I closely inspected the barrier coat and discovered that the surface was horribly textured – which I had not noticed when I was spraying – I left it for an hour in the hope that it would flow out. Some hope.

In the event, I quite accidentally discovered that my compressor was not giving me sufficient pressure to spray the thick barrier coat. I acquired a new tin, discovered it to be slightly less thick than the first one (I then warmed the paint to make it even thinner), and successfully sprayed this on – after, I might add, I'd spent two full days dry flatting the offending layer of barrier coat back!

When you come to spray a car which you have restored, various areas of the bodywork might be in the original paint, some will be in the primer in which repair panels are dipped, others might be bare steel. It's a lot of hard work, but there is no substitute for taking the lot back to bare steel, thoroughly de-greasing it, applying body filler as necessary and getting the lot into primer in one go.

BODYFILLER

Bodyfiller has a poor reputation amongst restoration armchair experts, whose knowledge is primarily book-learned and whose first-hand practical restoration experience can be negligible. Bodyfiller has a bad reputation because so many cowboy car repairers have in the past mis-used it; they slap filler over rusted steel, and the rust spreads underneath so that the filler eventually drops out – they slap on really thick layers to fill deep dents which should have been beaten shallow first, and because thick layers of bodyfiller cannot flex with the rest of the panel, they drop out. Applied directly on to clean, rust-free and preferably keyed (with a 40 grit abrasive disc) steel, bodyfiller can last the lifetime of the panel.

The key to preparing an area for bodyfiller is to firstly deal with any really deep dents – beating, pulling or levering them shallow – then to clean the area back to bright steel, to key it using a 40 grit disc (a 5.25" disc in an electric drill will suffice for this – the angle grinder is a tad too fierce!) and finally to de-grease it.

I usually take the time to go over the bodyshell and mark up any areas which are to be filled – a soft pencil will do for this. The alternative is to mix up some filler and then desperately seek out areas to be filled before the filler goes off! Stick to the recommended mix of filler and hardener, use an old spreader

to do the mixing rather than the clean one you intend to apply the filler with. Make fully sure that the filler/hardener has NO light or dark streaks in it, then set about spreading it onto the steel. Apply filler in thin layers – thick applications trap air bubbles which won't be apparent until you come to flat it. Apply sufficient layers until the filler is just proud of the desired level and extends slightly beyond the boundaries of the dent.

Tip: immediately after applying bodyfiller, I take the spreader to the hot water tap and clean all traces of filler off both it and my hands using soap and warm water. This leaves the spreader 'as new' – the alternative is to let the filler go off and then scrape it off the spreader, which inevitably marks the spreader so that it subsequently makes tram lines in the next layer of filler…

To flat filler, there is nothing to touch the air-powered long-bed sander – but these tools are expensive. The D/A sander is great for working curved surfaces but again, quite an expensive item to buy. I've fallen out with my electric random orbital sander due to its tendency to work concaves into the surface, and I now use the most basic tool known to man – a lump of wood. Well, to be precise, the 'lump of wood' is a 10" length of planed 4" x 2" softwood, around which I wrap half a sheet of 40 or 80 grit production paper (a long-lasting abrasive paper) – in other words, a sanding block. I prepared the wood by soaking it in water, so that any tiny splinters swelled, and then sanded the surface flat before painting it, so that it can also be used when wet flatting primer paint. Use finer than 40 or 80 grit abrasive on filler and it will clog up in seconds – omit the block and you'll simply sculpt concaves into the work.

Of course, a rigid sanding block isn't much use when you're working curved surfaces, which is where the DA sander reigns supreme. I simply wrap some cloth around the block and wrap the abrasive paper around this.

Some people flat filler using wet 'n dry – wet – but most bodyfillers are porous (they absorb moisture) and, because you have applied your filler onto bright steel, the very last thing you want to do is get the filler wet!

When the filler is close to the desired shape, I switch to 120 or 240 grit abrasive, to lose the deeper scoring from the rougher abrasives. I then scrub it with wire wool, which reduces the finer scratches left by the finer abrasive. Remembering that filler (excepting fillers made from aluminium particles) is porous, I prefer to get some primer onto it the moment flatting has ended.

SPRAYING EQUIPMENT

For many years, I toiled in vain to obtain a good finish spraying cellulose with a small tank compressor and spraygun. The results were usually passable, but not really good. The problems concerned a mixture of equipment shortcomings and user errors which were caused by the problems with the equipment, including finding a mixture of oil and water (a yellow emulsion) being spitted out of the gun onto the surface (despite fitting an oil/water trap), an inability to produce consistently high enough pressure to properly atomise the paint or give me a fan of more than 4" width, and the compressor overheating and cutting out when I was part-way across a panel. Some of these problems left me so exasperated that I took foolish short-cuts such as not applying sufficient topcoats for fear of anything else going wrong and ruining what finish I already had, or simply losing my temper, soldiering on regardless and making a real hash of things.

The oil/water contamination is apparent in the painted surface as thousands of tiny craters which have to be flatted out and re-covered. I reckon that you need at least a 2 HP motor and a 50 or preferably 100 litre tank to maintain the 50-60 psi needed to atomise the paint – my small compressor struggled to maintain 40 psi, so that the paint tended to splatter when the initial pressure had dropped (after one pass along a Beetle roof). The compressor would give me sufficient running time to spray maybe the roof, bonnet lid and one side of the car, then cut out. The edges of the paint would then dry whilst the compressor caught its breath, and this 'dry edge' is apparent through the topcoats.

I had three options: the first was to buy a much larger compressor and a good quality oil/water trap and spraygun, the second option was to go to my friend Em's and beg the use of his large compressor and high quality spraygun. The problem with both of these courses of action was that I was writing books on DIY restoration, and to do that properly, I had to persevere using DIY equipment rather than cheat by using pro-quality stuff. One further consideration made my third option the obvious choice. Spraying a car with cellulose entails running the compressor for perhaps fifteen minutes whilst each coat is applied, leaving the paint for twenty minutes to flash off, then applying the next coat. Because cellulose has a low pigment content, many coats are needed to build up a deep finish. Now, can you imagine living next door to someone who runs a compressor fifteen minutes on, twenty minutes off – for five to six hours at a time? The din from a compressor carries and, rather than drive my neighbours to take legal action against me, I took a chance and splashed out (I think it was £80 at the time) on an Apollo 400 High Volume, Low Pressure (HVLP) spray outfit.

The HVLP spray outfit consists of a small turbine unit, connected to the spraygun by a large diameter feed pipe. The turbine generates a large volume of low pressure air – and does so with no more noise than a household vacuum cleaner – which is sufficient to atomise the paint. In addition to making far less noise than a compressor and the fact that there is no chance of air and/or water contaminating the paint, the HVLP saves a lot of paint which would otherwise, with a conventional outfit,

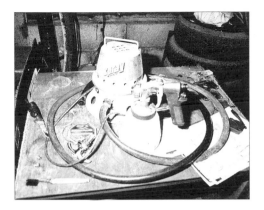

This little beastie is the smallest of the Apollo range of high volume, low pressure paint spray outfits. Although intended for limited DIY use, it will run all day, is very easy to use and far better than a small tank compressor for the DIY enthusiast.

Wet flatting primer. A little soap in the water helps prevent the abrasive paper from clogging while you wet flat primer. When you think the surface is perfect, spray on a thin coat of topcoat, then flat this back – you'll probably find lots of small scratches and holes to be filled with body stopper.

The legacy of a dent. As you flat, you'll cut back through various layers of paint, some of which might not be compatible with the topcoat you intend to use. A barrier coat prevents reaction.

Car masked for respray. Never rush masking-up – overspray can make or break the results. Ideally, you should re-mask after each coat of paint – allow the paint to harden, and removing the masking materials can also remove paint from adjoining surfaces. You should not use newspaper for masking, because the newsprint can dissolve and mar the paint finish. Don't you just love people who say "Don't do as I do, do as I say"?

It is always gratifying to see the bodyshell all in the same colour – even if it is only grey primer or even a barrier coat! It's time to bolt the rear wings on.

bounce back off the painted surface and fill the workshop with paint mist. As long as the paint viscosity is correct (this is critical with HVLP equipment), you get an 8" fan, meaning less passes of the gun per panel – less opportunity for things to go wrong. Another advantage is that the turbine will run happily day-in, day-out, and not cut out through overheating. Anyway, I bought it and it worked.

Following my advice, an old friend who is a

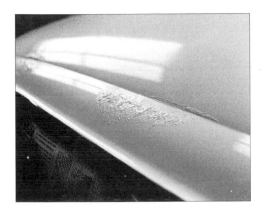

Aaaargh! Paint reaction! If you see blistering like this, then the offending paint has all got to come back off. I find that wire wool gives the quickest results – unlike abrasive papers, soft paint won't immediately clog it up.

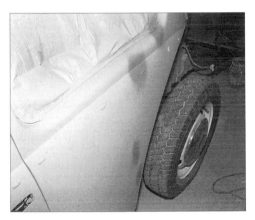

When you get paint reaction, you can opt to deal with specific areas, as I've done here, to spray the entire shell. One litre of barrier coat will do the whole exterior of a Beetle.

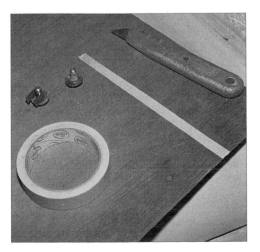

It is far easier to spray wings 'on' the car, but it is necessary to have a gap between the wings and the bodywork, to prevent paint from getting in the captive nut threads or on the wing bolts (do this and they'll be glued into position forever!). I fitted small spacers (bent strips of steel) to the two lowest bolts (to get the gap) and wrapped thin strips of masking tape around the rest of the bolts, to keep paint off the threads. Stick a length of tape onto a board, and cut strips using a craft knife.

Engine bay lid. I'm spraying the wings on the car, but the engine bay lid off so that I can get some paint up around the hinges area.

The car ready to spray. Note the old curtains wrapped around the wheels to keep overspray off.

When you've sprayed on the primer, it's back to wet flatting (left). To make the roof centre slightly easier to reach, let some air out of the tyres! Don't schedule this for the middle of winter – I did, and I can tell you that keeping your (wet) hand in contact with near-freezing steel makes your hand, wrist and forearm ache. Start off with 600 grit, move through 800 to 1000 or even 1200 grit if you want a decent finish. Expect things to go wrong – not just while you're spraying paint, but throughout the restoration. Saves disappointment when disaster strikes and heightens the joy when things occasionally go according to plan.

To avoid flatting straight through the primer, you need to be able to see what you're doing, which is not easy when the surface is covered in a mixture of paint dust and water. Use a windscreen wiper blade frequently to clear this from the surface.

professional restorer (and who already had top-quality conventional spraying equipment) bought a larger model from the Apollo range, and he has since not tired of telling me how good it is! Like me, he has come to appreciate that he can spray in a crowded workshop without paint settling everywhere, that he can still see in the workshop after spraying due to the absence of paint mist and that he can obtain first-class results as well. He says the Apollo is the best investment his company ever made!

This looks like topcoat (below) because it's so shiny, but it's primer. I followed up the last 'proper' coat with a coat of nearly neat thinners, which encouraged the surface of the primer to flow out properly. Saves on wet flatting time.

Attention to detail. Flatting the rain gutters and the line just inboard of the roof edge takes ages.

PAINT

If you are working 'by the book', primer paint should be preceded by etch primer which, as the name suggests, etches the surface of the steel and provides a great key for subsequent paint. There is a small problem with etch primer. It is one of the most dangerous substances you could possibly breathe in – full respiratory gear is essential, which means not only having the appropriate face mask, but also a compressor large enough to furnish air not only to paint with but also for you to breathe. Don't even consider using etch primer unless you have the right gear – it's simply not worth the risk to your health.

Rather than risk using etch primer, you can ensure that the metal to be sprayed is well keyed, so that the paint has something upon which to get a good strong grip. A fairly coarse abrasive disc – 80 to 120 grit – used in a DA or an electric drill will provide lots of lovely scratches and the paint will be there for good.

Cellulose is the most commonly used paint for DIY vehicle refinishing. Its good point is its fast drying time, so that there is less opportunity for winged insects, leaves and other nasties to land in the wet paint. Its bad points are fourfold: it has a low pigment content, and so many layers are needed to build up a good, deep lustre; its thinners react with most other paint types and can lift these; and its thinners (solvent) will space you out if you breathe them in. Finally, cellulose shrinks as it dries; any tiny scratches underneath will show through.

However, all of the shortcomings of cellulose are outweighed by its single advantage – the fast air-drying times. Professional sprayers have the luxury of proper paint booths in which they have full control of the environment – they control the temperature, the humidity, they filter insects and other air-born dross out of the air, they extract air-dried particles of paint. You probably – like me – have a leaky, draughty garage or workshop to spray

in. Your control of the environment probably extends to opening a door or window to get air flow or cool things down. You will probably – like me – use cellulose. In fact, when I was ready to order the paint for my own Beetle, my suppliers told me that they did not have a formula for mixing VW L50B – Diamond Blue – in any paint type other than cellulose. Depending on the year and colour of your Beetle, the choice of paint type might be thus dictated.

When the bodyshell is in primer, leave this to harden for two weeks, then spray on a very, very light coat of the top coat (a 'guide' coat). When this is air-dry, wet flatting can commence. The idea is to wet flat away the guide coat using 600 or preferably 1000 grit wet 'n dry. This removes high spots and also shows up any scratches, which you can fill using cellulose body stopper.

When the surface is as near-perfect as possible (or when your patience runs out), it's time to apply the top coats. Three litres of cellulose should suffice; buy three one-litre tins – they're easier to pour from without spillage – and make sure that you quote not only the colour but also the manufacturer's paint code when ordering.

To spray cellulose, firstly stir and stir and stir it – some pigments settle out in the bottom of the tin and, if you don't get this all back into suspension then the colour won't be right. Strain the paint to remove any stringy bits, then add thinners so that the paint is thin enough to spray. You can buy special viscosity cups which have a hole in the base; fill one of these with a paint/thinners mixture and the amount of time it takes to drain will tell you whether it is thinned sufficiently. A lot of bother – I thin it to the point at which it comes off the stirrer in droplets rather than in a continuous stream. To check whether it is thinned enough, try test spraying a small area – if it splatters it's too thick, if it runs it's too thin!

What do paint spraying, welding skills, riding a bicycle and learning to swim all have in

Primer. This area has previously been brush painted with primer, but not flatted before the topcoats went on. As soon as I started to flat the old topcoat, the primer broke through. The moral is ot wet the entire bodyshell with 1000 or preferably 1200 grit wet 'n dry before spraying on the topcoat. This also helps remove traces of oil or other surface contamination.

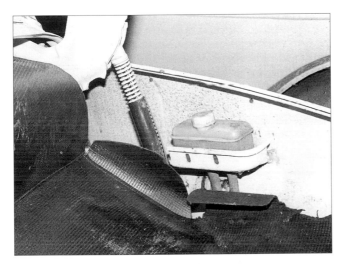

Small areas which are not on public display and which tend to rust – like the area around the brake fluid reservoir – can be (gently) brush painted, which saves the many hours of stripping components out and re-fitting them inherent in spraying such areas. If you're using cellulose, then bear in mind that (as my pal restorer Em Fryer is always telling me) so long as you've got plenty of paint on, you can always cut cellulose back to a good finish!

Captive threads tend to fill with paint when you spray the car. If you screw a bolt into a painted internal thread then it will stick there for ever, so it pays to clean out the threads. If you don't possess taps, cut a slot in a screw or bolt of the appropriate size and thread, and screw this into place – the slot acts as a reservoir for the paint, and the thread can come up like new. Even rusting can be removed from female threads in this way.

common? That's right – you cannot learn how to do them by reading a book. You can learn only from your mistakes, so practise on scrap steel before turning the spray gun on to your beloved Beetle.

If your paintwork turns out to be less than perfect, don't be too hasty in stripping all the offending paint off and starting again. Let the topcoats harden (six weeks for cellulose), then try to salvage it. Runs and sags can be gently flatted out using 1200 grit wet 'n dry (used wet with a sanding block), then gently cut and finally polished. Orange peel, dry spray and many other imperfections can be similarly flatted and cut away. Scratches, small holes and crazes may be salvageable – try filling the holes with cellulose putty (body stopper), then flatting and re-coating.

If, as is often the case, the problems turn out to be due to undercoats (runs or spots of overspray which, when you flat the topcoat, break through), then the best solution is to wet flat the offending areas (the water helps wash away any surface contamination) until the surface is smooth, then re-topcoat it – it's worth a try – you haven't much to lose!

PUTTING IT BACK TOGETHER

The final part of the restoration (rebuilding the restored car) should – in theory – be the most pleasurable. Not on your Nellie (USA translation – No Way). For a start, you have to work oh-so-carefully for fear of scratching that shiny new paintwork (you will scratch it – use a small artist's brush to repair the damage). Then there are usually problems with bought-in spares which turn out to be 'wrong' for your year and model of Beetle. Then there are problems with missing components and fittings. Then, if you overcome all these minor hassles, there's the electrics.

While the bodyshell and chassis are separated, it's silly not to fit a new clutch and release bearing, as well as check the starter gear, while access is so good. As you can see, all of these jobs are a real pain otherwise.

If you have to remove the engine, take the opportunity to check the condition of the clutch release bearing. It i s a good idea to renew this whenever you fit a new clutch, and in fact, sensible to renew the clutch if the engine has to come out for whatever reason.

Hope that you don't have complications like this! The clutch release bearing was damaged and had to come off. This could prove a real hurdle for a DIY restorer.

Offering up the clutch assembly. This is a competition clutch.

While the bodyshell is off, it's a good idea to renew the brake and fuel lines.

Here's Steve from BSW showing just how much fun it is to fit a Beetle engine. In fact, it's not so terrible a job once you've got the hang of it. Like so many jobs, though, expect the odd blood blister or skinned knuckle the first time you try it.

Engine bay tinware can be sprayed with high temperature resistant black paint. An aerosol can-full will suffice.

Before re-fitting the screens, you'll probably have to re-glue some of the headlining edges back down. Ensure that the glue you use is OK on cellulose paint if that is what you've sprayed the car with – some glues react with this paint.

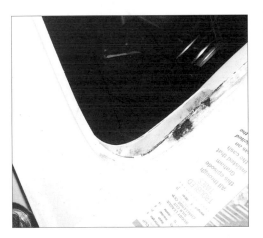

Predictable light surface rusting around the bottom of the windscreen aperture. I treated this with Dinitrol RC800 followed by brushed-on cellulose.

Before you fit the windscreen, make sure these drain holes are not clogged up with paint, otherwise, the lip will rust out!

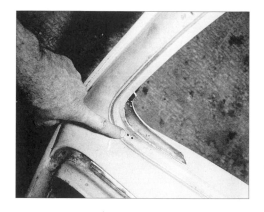

Fitting windscreen. Step One is to fit the new rubber. Don't, as I did, spend ages trying to work the glass into the wrong groove!

After fitting the rubber and chrome trim (a swine of a job), work a length of plastic-coated electric wire into the window aperture groove, and lubricate this with Swarfega hand cleaner – don't use washing up liquids because these can contain salts which will corrode the windscreen surround lip.

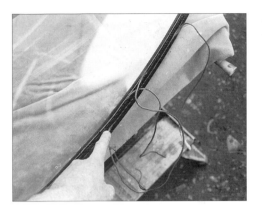

At the bottom of the screen, cross the ends of the wire over.

It is possible to fit a pre-McPherson front windscreen single-handed, but it is advisable to get some help. As you pull the rubber over the aperture lip by tugging on the wire, the screen tries to rise and to move sideways – your helper is there to stop it moving. Here, I've fitted the off-side and am almost at the top of the nearside pillar.

When the screen is in position, a few hefty clouts with the heel of your hand helps bed it down properly. This hurts your hand but, if you choose to use any implement to hit the screen with, don't be surprised if it breaks.

The outer lip had folded over at the bottom of the screen and was trapped – the sort of snag which can arise if you try to fit windows by yourself.

The solution was to push a length of stiff wire under the lip, then pull it out whilst pushing it forwards. Although I managed to fit the front screen single-handed, I did not succeed in fitting the rear (three helpers needed) and side (one helper needed) screens.

If you don't know your amp from your electron then read the introduction to fuel and electrics in the following chapter because, in order to trace electrical faults, you need to know what it is you're dealing with. Most eve-of-MOT electrical faults – non-functioning lights, brake lights that flash along with the indicators, that sort of thing – are caused by bad earth connections. Simple as that. If a fuse blows then the current which should be reaching the associated component (wiper motor etc.) is shorting to earth instead – never simply replace or – worse – uprate a blown fuse; if you do that you're risking starting an electrical fire. Disconnect the battery, read the following chapter, get hold of a test meter and track down that fault. Call in an auto-electrician if you get nowhere.

SURVIVING PROFESSIONAL RESTORATION

To the satisfied customer, the professional restorer is a mixture of magician, oracle and superhuman all rolled into one. To the professional restorer, the satisfied customer is someone to be tolerated and humoured and given an eventual fond farewell as they depart in a shiny restored Beetle with a smile on their face (and a hole in their bank balance).

To the disgruntled customer, the restorer is a shark, a charlatan; count your fingers after shaking hands with him. To the professional restorer, the disgruntled customer is a pain in the butt, a prying, whining, tight-wad who expects miracles on a minimal budget and whose car is in dangerously close proximity to that cutting torch – if he comes round here griping once more…

It clearly pays to end up a satisfied customer, a process which begins with finding the right restorer for your Beetle. When looking for a competent and honest restorer, there is no substitute for a recommendation from a satisfied customer or preferably several (just in case the 'satisfied customer' is the restorer's brother-in-law). Take a look at some restored Beetles; talk to the owners and, to find those, you only have to head for the nearest Beetle club branch or the next big Beetle event.

A few sad people, as we have already established, will not admit that some or all of a restoration was carried out by professionals,

It is usually necessary to replace the luggage and engine bay seal lips. Some pitting of the underlying steel is almost inevitable; clean this off with a cup brush in an angle grinder, and be certain to get the lot off and use weld-through zinc primer before spot welding the replacement lip on.

On of the least pleasant tasks is removing or re-fitting the transaxle – a strong argument for fitting it whilst the bodyshell is off!

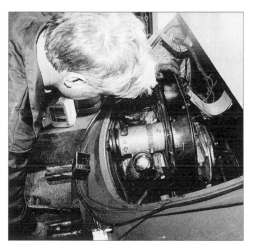

Fitting the engine can be accomplished single-handedly by an experienced person – if you've never done it before, get some assistance.

preferring to claim to have done it all themselves, though the vast majority of Beetle owners are honest, decent types who will happily give credit where it is due. People who are pleased with their car's restoration never miss a chance to show the car off, to luxuriate in the compliments paid by on-lookers. By the same token, the disgruntled customer is seething, vengeful and won't pass up any chance to tell anybody and everybody their views regarding the parentage and incompetence of the restorer who so obviously upset them.

But you have to be able to read in between the lines, to interpret whatever the satisfied and dissatisfied customers say. A satisfied customer could turn out to be a real dunderhead who doesn't know that the 'restorer' whose praises he is all too willing to sing used GRP and body filler to repair a hole in the flitch panel. A dissatisfied customer could turn out to be one of nature's pains in the butt – the kind of wholly unreasonable and very vocal 'professional complainer' dreaded by everyone whose job means that they have to deal with the General Public.

Temper whatever Beetle owners tell you about a restorer – good or bad – with your own conclusions about the standard of workmanship. To judge restored Beetles, you have to know something about restoration practices, which means reading everything you can about the subject.

The restoration trade hate armchair experts; good restorers, because the pure theory which forms the basis of the armchair expert's expertise usually bears little resemblance to actual workshop practice in the Real World, bad restorers because even the most badly-advised armchair expert can spot shoddy practice. Best not to divulge armchair expertise in any dealings with a restorer.

Look closely at areas where part-repair panels are commonly grafted in; the door skin lower sections and quarter panels, A and B post bottoms. There's nothing wrong with the use of such repair sections – what you're trying

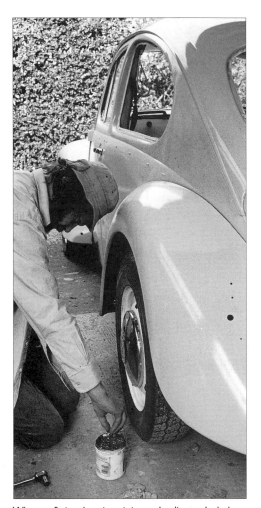

When re-fitting the wings, it is good policy to dunk the bolts in copper-based grease. Fail to do this, and you'll be lucky to ever get the wing off again!

to establish is whether they were poorly applied. Check for evidence of poor finishing (a visible line), paint bubbling or rusting along the join and for rivelling in the quarter panel. Check the door gaps and the shut lines of the luggage and engine compartment lids. Squat down in front of the car and check that the front end is true to the rest (quite a few Beetles

New indicator rubbers. I managed to force the spade connectors through the new rubber tube on the off-side, but the nearside rubber (from a different supplier) was too inflexible to allow this, so I cut off the spade connectors, threaded in the wire, then fitted new connectors.

Crimping tools are worth their weight in gold. Don't mess around trying to fit terminals with a pair of pliers when the correct tool for the job costs so little.

have rebuilt but skewed front ends). If, underneath the car or especially anywhere on the heater channels, you see a welded-on cover 'repair' patch or several then forget about using that restorer – no reputable restorer has any excuse for such shoddy practice.

A full 15,000 word guide to appraising Beetles is included in *Beetle – Preparation/Restoration/Maintenance* published by Osprey Automotive.

It pays to concentrate in your search on relatively local restorers – if you were to choose

one situated 200 miles from your home it won't be easy to keep an eye on progress during the restoration! Don't even consider a restorer who does not specialise – ideally exclusively – in the Beetle. Good Beetle restorers don't have problems finding work (my local Beetle specialist, for instance, is usually fully booked up for six months or more – it's worth the wait), and a restorer who has to take in cars other than Beetles to keep the workshop busy obviously hasn't gained much trade by personal recommendation on the Beetle 'grapevine'. Try

The one door trim was ragged around the window winder handle, and the hardboard was showing. I cut a small piece of vinyl out of an old seat and dyed this black, the idea being to try to work it into position under the torn vinyl. This was a complete failure – the dye rubbed off on my hands.

In the end, a paintbrush and some gloss black enamel paint provided an obvious solution and you'd have to look quite hard to discover the repair.

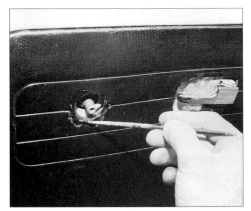

Don't forget to fit the tapered spring under the winder handle – many people do.

Fitting a new door seal proved problematic because I could not find a glue which was compatible with the cellulose paint I'd used on the car. You need glue only around the door lock area.

Bumpers. Old bumper bolts are liable to 'round' the square holes in the bumpers, and the only way to get them off is the chisel or grinder. I fitted cheap bumpers and, within a year, they had started to rust.

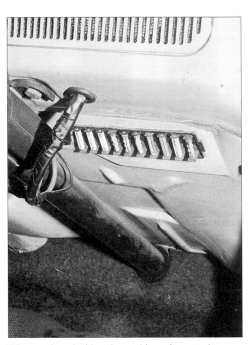

When you're rebuilding the car, blown fuses can be a real headache. If a fuse blows, disconnect the battery and use a multi meter to locate the earth leakage.

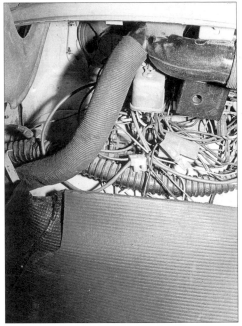

Yes – the electrics behind the dash are a real birds' nest. Before you plunge your hand into this tangle, take the precaution of firstly disconnecting the battery and take care not to inadvertently pull any spade connectors from their terminals.

to draw up a short-list of those who you feel able to entrust with the work and whose hourly charge does not resemble a telephone number, and prepare to do battle with them.

Only joking. You don't have to do battle with the restorers, only a little espionage. Under cover of being an ordinary citizen rather than a Beetle restoration armchair expert, visit each restorer and ask for a quotation for the restoration of your car. While the restorer circles your car sucking air between his teeth, shaking his head and scribbling yet more figures down on his notepad, take a look at the premises.

A good restoration workshop will possess the following. Beetles being restored. A Beetle-owning boss and preferably Beetle-owning staff. Plenty of room and light, and a water-tight roof. Good quality tools neatly and methodically stored away so that they can quickly be found when needed. Spot, Mig and gas welding equipment. A pit or preferably a car lift. Staff who don't smoke in the workshop and who use appropriate safety equipment, such as gauntlets and eye protection. Combustible materials stored safely away in an outside building. The very best businesses will also have a spares sales division, and therefore a full range of spares on site, all of which will have been bought in at trade prices.

A bad restoration workshop will house the following. A variety of jalopies in various states of decay or part-restored in and around the workshop. A 3" thick layer of filler dust on the

When starting to rebuild the car, complete the under-dash wiring and fit the instruments, switches, radio etc BEFORE fitting the fuel tank. Stand in the fuel tank aperture, and you won't get a sore back leaning deep into the luggage bay.

Engine bay lid drain tubes – not all Beetles are fitted with these; if yours is, them don't make the mistake of pushing the pipes in too far, or the water won't drain and, when you lift the engine bay lid, it will pour over the engine!

floor. Oil slicks everywhere. Cramped working conditions, poor lighting and a leaking roof. Poor quality tools strewn about the floor so that the staff waste hours looking for the right tool. Only gas welding equipment. Jumbo-sized tubs of body filler. Miserable or over-frivolous staff whose cigarette ends smoulder where they fall on the floor. Tins of thinners stored next to gas heaters.

Check out the work in progress. Ask yourself whether the appropriate rust-proofing measures, such as weld-though zinc primer for any overlapping or joddled joints are utilised, or whether the car can be expected to begin rusting within a twelvemonth of the restoration. Are quality repair panels used, are part-repair panels fitted where the full panel is really needed?

What about paintwork? Professionals really should have proper spray booths – if not, they might farm the topcoating out to a specialised company which does have all the facilities: ask.

After months in the workshop, 'Project' is ready for the MOT test, after which, the lanes of Worcestershire beckon.

Each restorer you visit should furnish an itemised estimate for the restoration. Beware of exceptionally low estimates, these are no more than an underhand means of securing the work, and the bill will inevitably rise part-way through the restoration. What normally happens is that the restorer 'overlooks' essential work when drawing up the estimate, but – surprise, surprise – 'discovers' it part-way through the restoration when the bodyshell is separated from the chassis and the hapless customer has no option other than to cough up the extra. Be very wary of low estimates. A very high estimate can come from a company which simply has too much work on and which is only prepared to squeeze your car into a busy schedule if you make it worth their while – it's not generally worth paying the extra.

You have to accept that the restorer might, in discovering a need for extra work part-way through the restoration and bringing this to your attention, be doing you a huge favour rather than ripping you off. If, for instance, when cleaning and painting the chassis the restorer discovered that the frame head lower closing panel was a repair panel which had been welded on top of the rotting original then, by bringing this to your attention, he would be allowing you the option of having it put right. He could alternatively ignore this huge bodge and complete the restoration to your satisfaction – in the fullness of time the frame head would rot out completely and you would be faced with a bodyshell-off semi restoration when the car failed its MOT.

Remember that an estimate is just that – an estimate (an educated guess, perhaps 'guesstimate' would be a more appropriate term) of the eventual cost of the restoration, based on what the customer tells the restorer regarding the desired standard of workmanship and of the completed car. It is essential that both you and the restorer know exactly what you, the customer, expect of the finished car. Unless you specifically agree certain details, such as the painting of the luggage compartment, the complete replacement of a body pressing rather than the use of a repair panel and so on, disputes can and do arise. Take time to go over the estimate with a fine tooth-comb and resolve any possible areas of misunderstanding before the work commences.

The estimate should list and separately price all components and repair panels, so check the prices against those in a current spares catalogue to see whether they intend to rip you off by over-charging for these. It should give the hourly labour rate and the total estimated hours for the job. If all you are offered is a vague total with the advice that the final bill could be lower, forget it.

A good Beetle restorer is always in demand, and so don't expect a restorer to be able to start work on your car immediately – unless a convincing explanation can be found such as a cancellation, then assume that the restorer is not terribly popular.

The restorer should offer to keep a photographic record of the work, which you can use as proof of the car's restoration should you ever come to sell it. Equally importantly, a photographic record of the restoration becomes a part of your Beetle's history, adding to its aesthetic and fiscal value.

A restorer who won't photograph the restoration obviously has too much to hide. A restorer who tries to put you off having the work photographed by hinting that it will add to the bill should be avoided.

You should have a standing invite to call in to see how the work is progressing – any restorer who tries to put you off checking up in this way has something which he does not want you to see and is to be avoided. When you do call, don't hang about too long, don't distract the people doing the work – remember that you are paying for their time, whether they are chatting to you or restoring your car!

PRO-AM RESTORATIONS

Most restorers adopt a fairly flexible attitude to the work they undertake; most are quite happy – for example – to take delivery of a bare shell after you have undertaken the stripdown at home, to carry out welded repairs and paintwork, and to return the shell to you for boxing up. This might wipe 40% off the restoration labour costs – if you do the paintwork, make that 60%.

Not all restorers will want to get involved in pro-am restorations, though, because they know from experience that, if they deliver a shell with a perfect paint job and it gets scratched back at the owner's premises during boxing-up, the owner will often seek to blame the company.

Alternatively, you can in effect 'manage' a professional restoration by farming out specific tasks to individual specialists, overseeing the lot from home. This can save money, but the problem is that each specialist will blame another if anything does go wrong, and it can prove impossible to pin the blame down to any of them when that happens.

The cheapest route to a professional-standard restored car is to keep it on your own premises and bring in mobile specialists – a welder, mechanic – as and when needed (when you get out of your depth). You can trailer the car to the best paintshop in the area and get a first-class paint job and, if you carry out most of the boring preparation work at home beforehand, at a fairly low cost.

CHAPTER FOUR

Surviving Breakdowns

For the first five to – in some cases – ten years of their lives, modern cars are even more reliable than the Beetle, but the reliability of the cars of the 1990s is held to ransom by an ever-greater sophistication and, as today's new cars age, it appears probable that their reliability will suffer simply because they will have so many extra old components to go wrong. Even some of the cars of the late 1960s and 70s were becoming so needlessly complicated that they seemingly became extinct as a species almost overnight – as component after component gave up the ghost and the cars were eventually scrapped by their unfortunate owners, when they came to realise that in meeting constant repair bills they were merely throwing good money after bad.

In contrast, the simplicity of the Beetle means that there are relatively few components which can give problems, which goes some way to explaining the Beetle's legendary (and lasting) reliability…

But Beetles can and do go wrong. Not too often, admittedly, but when your Beetle judders to a halt or refuses to fire up in the morning, you are in a far better position than the owners of modern cars in similar straits. The simplicity of contact breaker point and coil ignition rather than electronic or computer-controlled versions, of carburation rather than fuel injection (USA cars excepted) makes fault finding possible for ordinary folk like us. Pity the owner of a modern car which refuses to start – without thousands of pounds' worth of electronic diagnostic computer to hand to check the ignition system, without highly specialised equipment to test the fuel injection system, without replacements for expensive non-repairable sealed units – he or she is up an oft-navigated creek without a paddle.

Most fault-finding guides are rule-based and take the form of questions and answers, such as Is there fuel in the tank? If there is, then move on to the next question; if there is not, then you are advised to put some in – fascinating stuff. In an effort to make the guides easier to use, they are often presented as flow charts, meaning long series of questions and answers; IF symptom one, AND symptom two, BUT symptom three, THEN the fault is this. There are two problems with this approach. Firstly, breakdowns usually occur on the one occasion when you've forgotten to pack the fault-finding guide in the car. Secondly, there are hundreds of such rules – simply too many rules to be memorised.

My approach is to learn how things work because, if you do understand how something works, then you can usually work out for yourself why it sometimes doesn't.

AN INTRODUCTION TO FUEL AND ELECTRICS

The two major causes of non-starting engines and roadside breakdowns are problems in the electrical (ignition) and fuel delivery systems; it is far easier to trace non-starting and breakdown faults if you have a basic understanding of how these work. Of the two, the fuel delivery system is the simpler, so we'll take a look at this first. The following is not a treatise on the workings of the automobile, but considers only specific areas which typically contribute to breakdowns.

CARBURETTORS

Petrol is stored in the fuel tank and drawn by a mechanical (integral with the engine) pump, which pushes it into a fuel bowl in the carburettor. A float within the fuel bowl operates a

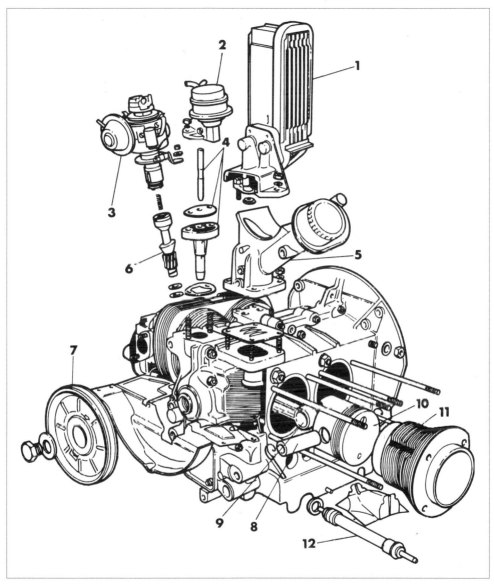

The workings of the Boxermotor. Refer to this as you read this chapter. (Diagram courtesy Autodata). 1. The oil cooler radiator is as important as the radiator in liquid cooled cars. 2. The fuel pump with (4) its push rod assembly. 3. The distributor with (6) its drive shaft. 5. The generator pedestal (incorporating the oil fill neck). 7. Crankshaft pulley (with timing marks). 8. Piston pin (9) connecting rod and (10) piston. 11. Cylinder barrel and (12) pushrod, which operates the rocker gear and opens the valves.

Choke throttle lever engaged.
The choke throttle lever opens the
throttle according to engine temperature; first thing in the morning,
it raises tickover speed.

Choke throttle lever off. The
choke control raises the stepped
throttle lever as the engine warms
and is able to tick over normally.

valve when the bowl becomes full, so cutting
off the supply of fuel and preventing the
engine from receiving too much fuel, which
means flooding the cylinders. If the cylinders
were to flood, the spark plug ends would
become soaked and could not spark to ignite
the mixture.

As the engine turns over, air is drawn down
into it through the carburettor throat, in which
the various jets are situated. A jet is simply an
opening through which petrol can be drawn,
and the different jets supply fuel according to
the engine's needs at any time. As air rushes
through the carburettor throat, its density and
hence its pressure drops, and the low pressure
air draws tiny droplets of petrol from the jets,
so that a mixture of fine droplets of petrol and
air enter the combustion chambers. This mixture is ignited by a sparking plug to provide the
energy to power the car.

Different proportions of petrol droplets and air are required at different times. The amounts of air and petrol are defined by their weight rather than volume. For starting a cold engine, the ratio is around 1:1, that is, for every ounce of air which enters the cylinders, you need an ounce of petrol (don't forget that petrol is far more dense than air – it takes a huge volume of air to weigh an ounce). When the choke is operating and the mixture is this rich, miles per gallon will be in single figures. Once the engine has warmed up, however, the mixture can be made much weaker, so it no longer needs the choke. The choke on Beetles is automatic, and operates according to the temperature in the engine bay. You get about one minute's worth of choke, then you're on your own and you may find that you have to keep the revs up to prevent the engine from stalling until it has more completely warmed up!

For maximum miles per gallon during steady cruising, the mixture is ideally weakened to nearer 1:15 to 1:16 – one part petrol to sixteen parts air. This mixture is sufficient to allow the car to maintain a speed, but too weak when extra power is required – i.e.., for overtaking – and so extra fuel is again required, provided by another jet which has its own little pump linked to the throttle spindle. Put your foot down and the pump gives a temporarily enriched mixture to throw the car forwards with searing acceleration (well, not quite!).

The Beetle is fitted with one of a number of fixed jet carburettors and, although they differ in detail (the later ones became more complex) they all deliver the various mixture strengths in the same basic manner.

The choke is a butterfly flap situated above the jets, which cuts the amount of air drawn into the engine, so that a higher proportion of fuel is drawn into the mixture in relation to the quantity of air, giving the 'rich' mixture to help start the engine on cold mornings.

The throttle flap is situated on the engine side of the jets so that, as it opens and it allows more air into the engine, more fuel is drawn in proportion. To re-cap, one jet supplies fuel for idling, a larger jet comes into operation at higher engine revolutions, and the third, with its own pump, supplies the extra fuel for that neck-snapping acceleration.

The fuel system also contains fuel filters, which trap any foreign bodies in the fuel, such as tiny rust flakes from the inside of the fuel tank and any objects which might fall into the fuel tank filler neck when the car is being re-fuelled.

FUEL INJECTION

From the mid-1960s onwards, concern about atmospheric pollution caused by motor cars resulted in efforts by motor manufacturers to reduce that pollution. Fuel tank breathers were fitted with carbon filters to scrub out hydrocarbons from evaporating petrol, fuel delivery systems had retrieval systems, air was pumped into exhaust manifolds to burn off un-burnt and partially burnt fuel, and crankcase breathers funnelled hydrocarbon fumes into the inlet manifold, so that they would burn in the engine.

The levels of hydrocarbons in the atmosphere most especially in and around some large North American cities reacted with strong sunlight and caused a photochemical smog, which led to the introduction of legislation to reduce the levels of hydrocarbons emitted from cars. Also high on the pollution agenda were other polluting substances which are a by-product of the internal combustion engine – Carbon Monoxide (CO – a quite deadly gas) and Oxides Of Nitrogen (NOX). These can be dealt with by burning them in the exhaust manifold, but the technique does tend to rob the engine of power. In Europe, most efforts to reduce pollution were aimed at improving the efficiency of the combustion process, very often retaining carburettor fuel delivery. In North America, where pollution problems in limited areas were more serious, some of the manufacturers opted for fuel injection systems.

Fuel injection systems allow the amounts of fuel being delivered to vary more precisely according to demands than can carburation systems. There are two benefits to this; greater power can generally be achieved and exhaust emissions can be more precisely controlled. The down-side of fuel injection is its greater complexity in comparison with simple, user-repairable carburettors.

Fuel is pumped from the tank as in carburation systems but the injection system incorporates an accumulator (or regulator) which maintains the constant high pressure needed (which typically ranges from 25 psi to 100 psi depending on the type of injection system), because fuel atomisation is dependent upon it being pumped under high pressure through a jet (single point) or jets (multi-point). The accumulator also smoothes out individual fuel pump pulses to maintain a constant pressure, and it maintains some fuel pressure when the engine is switched off, so that adequate pressure is forthcoming immediately the engine is re-started.

There are essentially two types of fuel injection system. The earlier systems by and large employed simple mechanical operating methods common to contemporary diesel injection systems. An air flow sensing plate and lever operate the mechanical mixture control unit which enriches or weakens the mixture according to the amount of air being drawn into the engine. The mixture control unit contains a valve mechanism which is driven from the engine and which allows fuel into each injector as and when needed.

Electronic fuel injection systems incorporate an Electronic Control Unit (ECU). This is in effect a simple digital computer which reacts to electronic input signals from the distributor (to control injector opening timing), the accelerator pedal, the air temperature sensor and air pressure sensor, and which controls the various injectors' opening times and durations (electric,

by solenoids), plus an extra air valve, which effectively bypasses the throttle butterfly, allowing a very lean mixture into the engine on the overrun.

ELECTRICS

The electrical system is more complicated to explain, and we'll start at the very beginning by looking at what electricity is. You can't smell or see it – so just what is electricity? Think of a length of copper wire at the atomic level. Each atom is surrounded by many orbiting electrons – as the moon orbits the earth – some of which are held in orbit more strongly than others by their nucleus. When no electrical current is flowing, some of these less strongly held electrons become detached from their atoms and fly off to collide with other atoms which, in turn, can have one of their electrons knocked out of orbit. This movement of electrons is random BUT, when the two ends of the wire are connected to a battery, there exists a glut of electrons at one end and too few at the other, a potential difference which causes electrons to flow through the wire from one terminal to the other – in other words, the random flights of electrons have been replaced with a steady and directional flow.

This seems as good a time as any to digress slightly and mention that when a copper wire which is part of a circuit passes through a magnetic field, a small current is generated and, the longer the length of wire, the greater the current. This is how electricity is generated by the dynamo or alternator – a long length of coiled-up wire passing through a strong magnetic field.

So electricity can be defined as a controlled flow of electrons, but how is this put to use? For our purposes, there are two side-effects of electrical current flow of interest; electricity flowing through a material generates 1). heat and 2). magnetic fields. Heat is generated when the flow reaches an area of resistance – a material whose atoms hold on to their electrons rather more tightly than do conductive materials such as copper, gold and silver. The resistive metals used in light bulbs are the most obvious example; run electricity through them and they get hot – so hot, in fact, that they give out bright light. Were they not surrounded in an inert gas inside the glass bulb which prevents combustion from occurring then they would burn through in a fraction of a second. Another areas of resistance are corroded connections, a length of damaged wire with reduced cross sectional area or a wire of too-small a cross sectional area – if it allows electricity to pass through but restricts the flow then it will become hot.

Whilst on the subject of wires, the cross sectional area of wire must increase in accordance with the quantity of electricity it will have to handle. A side-light wire carries only a small current and so is of thin section wire whilst the starter motor wires carry a huge current (300 to 400 amps) and so they are very thick. If too much electricity is drawn through too thin a wire, the wire will quickly become hot, burn off its insulation and eventually melt.

Magnetism is another matter. When current flows through a wire, a weak magnetic field is created around the wire. This is too low in power to be of any automotive use, but if the length of wire is coiled up so that a great length of wire occupies a small volume, then the strength of the field is increased and can do a lot of work.

The best illustration of how electro-magnetic force is put to use is the starter solenoid, which has an electro-magnet which, when power flows through its coil, generates sufficient magnetic force to pull a metal bar until it touches two hefty electrical contacts to complete another electric circuit, but one which requires very high levels of energy – the starter motor circuit. The starter solenoid is an electrically powered switch. The first section of the ignition system (that is from the ignition switch to the starter solenoid coil) carries only small

currents, which is important not only because it saves having to run yards of heavy-duty cable from the engine bay to the ignition switch but also for safety reasons. You turn on the ignition and the ignition circuit is energised, turn the key a little more and the starter solenoid completes a heavy-duty circuit to turn the starter motor.

Onto the battery. Most people believe that the car battery stores electricity – wrong! The car battery houses metallic and chemical substances which, when a load (a light bulb, wiper or starter motor etc.) is connected, begin a reversible chemical process. Inside the battery are a number of cells each containing two dissimilar metal plates in a weak acid solution (electrolyte). When you throw a switch and complete the circuit between the two terminals, electrons flow from one type of plate to the other, changing the chemical composition of each and in the process generating a small electrical current of just over two volts. A six volt battery contains three cells, a twelve volt battery contains six.

The chemical process in a car battery is reversible; that is, when the generator (dynamo or alternator) creates an electrical current, some is fed to the battery and reverses the process so that the two metals return to their former composition, 're-charging' the battery.

To save on wiring, the chassis and body of the car, being composed of metal which conducts electricity, are substituted for one of the wires needed to complete a circuit. The body in this respect is known as the 'earth' (UK) or 'ground' (USA). So, a feed wire runs from a battery terminal, through a switch to a device – a light bulb or whatever – through the device, into the bodyshell and back to the other battery terminal, which is connected to the body by the earth strap. Whilst on the subject of earths, electric currents in a circuit actively seek these out because they are the channel of least resistance back to the battery – if a wire leading to a light bulb, for instance, shorts to earth, then the current will take this easier route rather than pass through the light bulb, in the process, drawing excessive current and blowing a fuse or damaging the wiring.

A fuse is a length of single-strand wire with no insulation and of a specific thickness such that, if too high a current flows through it, it very quickly becomes hot enough to melt and therefore break the circuit before damage occurs to the wiring. Fuses are incorporated into circuits to protect the wiring and components which, if the fuse did not break the circuit when it became overloaded, would overheat and possibly cause an electrical fire. A blown fuse is not a fault in itself, but a symptom of a fault elsewhere in the circuit – most usually a short to earth – that is, a part of the wiring with damaged insulation or perhaps an un-insulated terminal is touching earth so that electricity flows directly to earth rather than through the load (light bulb, wiper motor, radio etc.). When a fuse blows, disconnect the battery, trace and rectify the actual fault before replacing the fuse and NEVER fit a fuse of a higher amperage rating to try and 'cure' a fault – you'll only risk starting an electrical fire.

An electrical fire is not a pleasant experience. I can tell you from personal experience that a fire within the passenger compartment takes around thirty seconds to fill the compartment with black, choking smoke. That's how long it took me to disconnect the battery and avoid seeing my car going up in flames. A friend was not so lucky, and when his car suffered an electrical fire, he sensibly chose to put as much distance as possible in between the burning car and himself; the fuel tank exploded first (the rear hatch landed some distance away), followed by a louder bang as the glass sunroof exploded, and the car was a burnt-out wreck within minutes. I repeat, NEVER fit a fuse of a higher amperage rating to try and 'cure' a fault – you'll only risk starting an electrical fire.

We've looked at electricity, wires and batteries; what next? The ignition system (which causes more breakdowns than any other reason except running out of petrol!).

When you operate the ignition key, the ignition circuit energises a coil of wire called the primary winding within the body of the ignition coil. Also within the coil is a secondary winding called – wait for it – the secondary winding, which has many times more individual coils than the primary winding. A strong magnetic field builds up around the primary winding (it is an electro-magnet) and, when the circuit which feeds it is broken, the magnetic field collapses and induces an electrical charge in the secondary winding. The secondary winding is not far off a mile in length – far longer than the primary winding, which 'steps up' the voltage. The voltage created when the magnetic field collapses is many times higher than the twelve volts of the primary winding – 25,000 volts, in fact, which is sufficiently high to be able to jump across small gaps to find an earth. When electricity jumps a gap like this, a spark is created – that's how spark plugs work. Both coil windings are cooled by oil contained within the coil casing. The coil can overheat – incidentally – and its case split if the ignition is left switched on for long periods with the points closed and the engine not running. So far so good.

Inside the distributor, the points are closed and it is these which complete the circuit to earth which energises the primary winding in the coil. As the engine turns over, one of the distributor drive shaft cam lobes opens the points, so breaking that circuit, so that the magnetic field of the primary winding breaks down, generating the high voltage in the secondary winding, which immediately looks for an earth, escaping into the main coil to the distributor High Tension (HT) lead. The primary circuit may have been broken by the points opening, but the residual electric charge (around 12,000 volts) in the primary coil is quite strong enough to jump across the open contact breaker points to find an earth. As you will remember, areas of high resistance generate heat, and the air gap in the points is one such area.

Because having electricity jump across the points between two thousand and ten thousand times a minute (at engine revolutions of 1,000 rpm and 5,000 rpm respectively) would rapidly burn away the points, the distributor is fitted with a condenser. This contains two rolled-up sheets of conductive metal, separated by an insulator, so that the two cannot touch. The residual electric charge in the primary coil doesn't know this, and rushes into the condenser thinking that it is an earth instead of jumping the gap between the points, so saving the points. Once the charge gets into the condenser, it realises it's been duped (pretty dumb, these electrical charges) and, because the points will by then have closed again to complete the circuit, it turns around and heads back for the primary winding and helps energise it ready for the next time that the points open.

While all this is happening, the rotor arm in the distributor is whizzing round and round, past the terminals in the distributor cap to which the sparking plug high tension leads are connected. As it approaches a terminal the points have opened and the 25,000 volts are headed towards it up the main high tension lead. The high tension lead from the coil tower (along which the charge from the winding is running) leads via the centre of the distributor cap and a carbon contact to the metal strip on the top of the rotor arm, and the charge runs down the strip and jumps across to the now adjacent sparking plug high tension lead terminal, then heads off in the direction of the spark plug, trying to find an earth to complete the circuit. When it gets there, it finds that it has to jump yet another gap (the spark plug gap) to get to earth, in so doing, providing the spark to ignite the fuel/air mixture within the cylinder. Pretty straightforward?

Now let's couple this information with a brief description of how the engine works.

Each of the four cylinders contains a piston and two valves. The piston rises and falls within the cylinder as the crankshaft turns, being connected to the crank by a connecting rod (con rod). As the piston falls, the inlet valve (connected to the carburettor) opens, allowing the mixture of air and fine particles of petrol to be sucked into the cylinder. The inlet valve closes and the piston rises, so compressing the mixture to around an eighth or ninth of its original volume. Just before the piston reaches the top of its travel (called Top Dead Centre or TDC), the spark plug ignites it, and the mixture begins to burn so that, by the time the piston has started to travel downwards again, the energy from the burning fuel pushes it, turning the crank and, in turn, moving the other three pistons within their cylinders.

As the piston again begins to rise, the exhaust valve opens and allows the burnt exhaust gas to escape into the exhaust manifold, heat exchangers and finally the silencer. The gas is still highly compressed as it leaves the cylinder and, if no silencer were fitted it would cause a very loud bang – if the silencer has a rusted hole in it, you'll hear the bang! The exhaust valve then closes, the inlet valve opens, the piston falls and the cycle is repeated.

There are four piston strokes; induction (drawing in the mixture), compression (compressing the mixture), ignition (burning the mixture) and exhaust (expelling the burnt gasses), and hence this is known as a four stroke engine. The Beetle engine has four cylinders, two each side of the crankshaft, and the engine is a horizontally opposed four cylinder, or – from the German – 'boxermotor'.

We have established that the strength of the air/fuel mixture varies according to the needs of the engine; idling, at speed and when accelerating. The other thing that varies is the ignition timing – the precise point at which the spark plug fires.

Early motor cars ran on unleaded fuel; this is a rather volatile liquid, prone to burning far too quickly to be of use – it burns too quickly to provide a good thrust to the piston throughout its power stroke, and the point of ignition and hence the start of the burn – has to be retarded (it has to occur later in the cycle).

In order to slow down the burn, lead was added, which slowed the mixture burn from around 200 metres a second (unleaded) to five metres a second and hence allowed the ignition to be advanced and the burn to commence earlier in the cycle and last longer, giving greater power.

Advancing the ignition thus gives greater power, and the ignition timing is varied in accordance with requirements in two ways. Firstly, two weights within the distributor body react to centrifugal force and advance the ignition as the engine revolutions increase, giving more advanced timing at higher speed. Secondly, in order to provide greater power during acceleration, a vacuum pipe from the inlet manifold (which contains low pressure mixture) is connected to the distributor and gives a further advance.

That is how the engine in your car works.

BREAKDOWNS

FLAT TYRE

Before looking at fault finding, perhaps we should begin with a simple wheel change to get into the swing of things. Most drivers will suffer a punctured tyre at some point in their motoring careers, and those who have never changed a wheel might care to take the precaution of practising doing so in the comfort and safety of their own driveway in preparation for the time they have to do it For Real at the roadside.

Firstly, although you should never in normal circumstances drive a car which has a flat tyre, do get the car to a place of safety (driving as slowly as possible) before stopping. On the motorway this is the hard shoulder. On ordinary roads, don't drive miles looking for a lay-by, because the tyre will come off the rim and

Wheel change. If you've never had to change a wheel, it's worth practising in the safety of your own driveway – better than having to learn how to do it on the motorway hard shoulder! Lever off the hub cap. and slacken the wheelnuts before raising the car.

you'll destroy both tyre and wheel; find a straight section of road where other motorists can see you in plenty of time – never stop on a bend in the road. If you have a warning triangle or anything else which will warn drivers to slow down before they reach you, put it out. If your car is fitted with hazard warning lights, switch them on. At night, at the very least leave your side-lights on.

Get the spare wheel out and check that it's inflated properly. Engage the handbrake and place the car in gear. If you can find a couple of stones (or keep chocks in the car) for the front wheel which is to remain on the ground

If you don't possess a wheelbrace, a 19mm cranked ring spanner will do to slacken the wheelnuts. Don't over-tighten them afterwards.

then use them. Slacken the wheel nuts, then jack up the offending side of the car, using the reinforced jacking point provided mid-way along the heater channel underside.

Remove the wheel nuts, pull the wheel off, offer up the spare and re-fit the wheel nuts. Tighten these until the wheel is securely held, then lower the car to the ground and remove the jack. The wheel nuts now have to be finally tightened, and many people don't seem to know how much to tighten them – don't overdo it by jumping up and down on the end of the wheelbrace – remember that you will have to get them off again – firm pressure with your arm muscles will be perfectly sufficient. It is as well to check the tightness of wheel fixings after having driven the car for a few miles.

ENGINE WON'T START

The least traumatic place to suffer a breakdown is on the drive at home, and happily, this is where the majority of breakdowns reportedly occur. Carry out the simplest checks first and leave the fancy stuff till later.

NOTE 1: Where the following information relates to fuel delivery problems, it pertains primarily to carburettor-equipped Beetles: problems with fuel injection systems really demand professional attention. Before booking your injected Beetle in for a diagnostic test, though, do take the time to go over the ignition system just to make sure that the 'fuel' problem isn't caused by ignition faults – many are. Also, check valve clearances, and check for engine air induction; because the inlet manifold air flow determines the amount of fuel which is injected, air induction fools the system into thinking that less fuel is needed than is actually the case.

NOTE 2: Before looking at non-starting faults, take note that when starting a car fitted with a fixed-jet carburettor from cold, the ONE thing which you should NEVER do is pump the throttle pedal while the starter motor is turning the engine. The choke has already enriched the mixture to around 1:1 and pumping the throttle pedal pumps neat fuel into the manifold. This soaks the ends of the spark plugs so that they cannot ignite the mixture. If this happens, remove the plugs and dry their ends.

ENGINE REFUSES TO TURN OVER

If the ignition light fails to come on then you've either got a completely discharged battery (unlikely) or a poor terminal connection. It could be a disconnection within the ignition primary circuit; more on this later, but for now, check the battery connections – the most likely cause. Remove the terminals (ALWAYS earth

If the ignition light glows, if the headlights, wipers and so on all work but the starter motor won't, there's a chance that battery terminal corrosion is the culprit. Clean the posts before trying anything fancy.

strap first), clean the battery posts and terminals with emery cloth, smear a little petroleum jelly on both and replace the terminals (earth strap last). Note; the reason why the earth strap should always be removed first and reconnected last is that, if you were to touch a spanner between the live terminal and ANY part of the bodywork with the earth strap connected, you would effectively short out the battery – with potentially disastrous results.

If the ignition light dims as the key is turned but no noise emanates from the starter motor, also check the battery connections. A loose or corroded connection can in some instances supply enough power for, say, the ignition primary circuit or even the headlights, but not enough to turn the starter motor. Also check the earth strap/bodywork connection for tightness and corrosion.

If the connections are good, the chances are that the battery is run down, meaning either that it is in poor condition and unable to hold a charge, that you left the lights switched on overnight or that the generator is not delivering a full charge. You can check whether the battery is nearly flat by switching on the headlights, judging their brightness, then turning on the windscreen wiper motor and seeing whether the lights dim further. Check the electrolyte level; if it is substantially down then the generator is probably over-charging the battery and boiling off the electrolyte – in the case of a dynamo, the regulator needs attention, alternators should be exchanged.

Whilst you can bump start the car or use jumper leads to get a car with a flat battery going, you should not travel anywhere other than to a place of repair unless you possess a multi meter and are able to check that the battery is being charged. Check with the engine running, with the engine running plus headlights, wipers on; set the meter to show voltage in the range 12 to 15 volts; anything much less than 13.6 volts indicates that the battery is being under charged, any reading much over

that level is over-charging – the voltage stabiliser should be exchanged.

If the battery seems OK, check the connections to the starter solenoid and the starter motor. This unfortunately means lying down and using a torch for illumination. If you don't want to get dirty, have an assistant operate the ignition switch whilst you listen for the starter solenoid 'click'. The solenoid, as we have already established, is an electrically operated switch which carries the huge current needed by the starter motor and which is activated by a very small current from the ignition switch. If it isn't operating, check that the thin wire has not come off its terminal and that the spade connector does not have internal corrosion which can act as insulation; if not, try giving the body of the solenoid a sharp tap with the handle of a large screwdriver or similar (ignition OFF, car out of gear – keep clear of moving parts just in case), and try again. If you have a test lamp, you can check whether current is reaching the solenoid. If power is there but the solenoid won't work, you could bump start the car to get it going but – because you would have no means of re-starting the engine if it conked out at the first set of traffic lights – you should do this only in order to drive the car to a nearby place of safety or repair.

If the solenoid is operating (you can hear it click), then the starter motor may be jammed. If so, place the car in fourth gear (ignition OFF), disengage the handbrake and rock the car forwards and backwards, which can often free a jammed starter. Alternatively, give the body of the motor a clout with a wooden mallet. If the engine still won't turn over, you'll have to replace the solenoid or replace/repair the starter motor as appropriate – either way, you ain't going anywhere. The problem could be cured with new starter motor brushes or pinion, or in the worst scenario it could necessitate replacement of the flywheel ring gear, so seek professional advice.

If the battery and terminals are OK and the

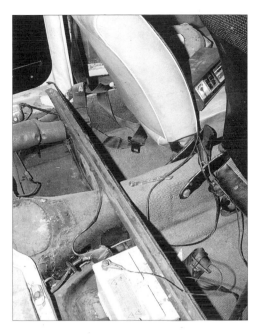

Battery on charge. Most battery chargers seem to pump about 2 amps into the battery, so that it takes ten hours' charging to get 20 amp hours in. Ideally, the battery should be removed from the car; they give off explosive fumes during charging, so it's not a good idea to charge them in a confined space. I'm just giving the battery a couple of hours' worth before starting the engine after a few weeks disuse.

Battery charge. Set the meter to read volts in the range 12-24V, (left) then connect it to the battery when the engine is running. Check the charge voltage both with everything switched off and on (lights, wiper etc).

Starter and solenoid connections. Before grovelling around in the dirt underneath the car, try operating the ignition switch and listen for the gentle 'click' from the starter solenoid.

ignition lamp fails to illuminate, then there is a disconnection within the ignition primary circuit. You can buy simple electrical testers consisting of a bulb, holder and earth wire for a few pounds, and one of these will enable you to check whether power is reaching the various parts of the circuit. You will also need a wiring diagram, in order to be able to see which wires belong to which circuit. You will find wiring diagrams within any workshop manual and in *Beetle Restoration/ Preparation/ Maintenance*.

ENGINE TURNS OVER BUT WON'T FIRE

Remember – don't pump the throttle – if you did, slap yourself on the wrist then remove the spark plugs, dry the ends, and try again. Otherwise, don't just sit there churning the engine over – all you'll accomplish by this is running the battery flat. CLEAN HANDS. Is there fuel in the tank? Is there an aroma of petrol from the exhaust tail pipe just after the engine has been turned over? – if so, fuel is reaching the engine and the fault probably lies with the ignition. Turn the ignition switch off and raise the engine bay lid.

You're going to have to get your hands dirty. IGNITION. Check the connections at either end of the main HT lead running from the coil to the distributor cap. Check the low tension circuit wires attached to the coil, and remake any poor connections. Check the high tension leads and distributor cap – if these have moisture on them then dry them off because they are allowing the charge which should go to the spark plugs to go to earth instead – and spray or preferably use a cloth to wipe on a thin coating of light oil and then try again to start the car.

If the engine still refuses to fire, switch off the ignition, pull the main HT feed from the distributor cap and hold this gently (if you possess the proper insulated pliers for the job – otherwise, try to tape it into position) a fraction of an inch from a good earth, well away from the fuel supply and the spark plug holes. Get an assistant to turn the engine over for a couple of seconds and observe whether a spark can be seen to jump between the HT lead and the earth – accompanied by an audible clicking

Using test bulb on ignition circuit. Coil test. Always carry out the easiest tests first. If there's no spark, check that power is reaching the coil.

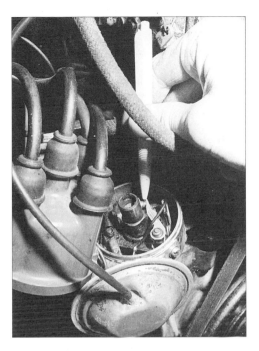

Alternatively, you can easily check for points splash. With the ignition switched on, levering the points open will result in a 'splash' (flash) if the ignition primary circuit is energised. If you get a real 'crack' as the points open then the condenser needs replacing.

Here, I'm disconnecting the low tension lead from the condenser, so that I can use the multi meter to check whether the condenser is faulty (whether it is acting as an earth). It is far from unknown for condensers to develop intermittent faults and, if the engine misfires intermittently and no fault can be found within the high tension circuit, try renewing the condenser.

Checking for a spark at the plug. A spark plug or lead can give you a nasty belt, so either hold the plug against an earth using insulated pliers or tape it there. These engine bay side panel lugs make good earths – well away from the spark plug holes.

sound. If not then either the coil or its feed is probably the cause. If there is a spark, then (ignition switch off) replace the HT lead in the distributor cap, remove the distributor cap and inspect it minutely for cracks which could contain moisture. Also check for signs of arcing – rough-edged black lines which contain carbon which forms a highly conductive path for electricity and channels it away from the correct spark plug. A temporary repair can be effected by scratching out the carbon, but the distributor cap should be replaced. Check that the points open and close freely and that their contacts are clean and not heavily pitted. If the points are dirty, clean them and try to start the engine.

When starting a car from cold, more than at any other time, the rich fuel/air mixture in the cylinders needs a good, strong spark from the plugs. Loose plug end fittings cause a loss of electrical energy to the sparking plugs and hence a weak spark, so check that the end fittings are all tight. If these are found to be loose, remove the spark plugs and dry off their ends – they will be covered with petrol.

Remove and check the spark plugs visually for obvious damage such as cracked ceramics, for heavy carbon deposits (wire brush this off, and make a note to have the carburation set – the engine is running too rich), sticky black deposits (clean off but make note to investigate at the first opportunity why oil is finding its way into the cylinders – could be broken or worn piston rings, valve stem to valve guide clearance), glazing (engine running far too hot – get professional advice and don't run the engine in this state), and correct gap (adjust). Then place each plug in turn in its lead and tape it to a good earth away from the fuel delivery system, carburettors and plug holes (or hold it using the proper insulated pliers) and have the engine turned over to see whether there is a spark. Absence of a spark could be due to a faulty plug or lead, so try apparently faulty plugs on other leads to establish which is

at fault: replace any faulty plugs or leads.

FUEL. Carburettor Beetles Only. Fuel delivery problems are far less common causes of non-starting engines than ignition faults. It cannot be said too often so I'll reiterate – the most common fuel-related non-starting problem is flooding of the engine caused by pumping the throttle pedal whilst the engine is turning over. Pumping the throttle pedal pumps neat petrol into the carburettor throat but, because the choke will be 'on' during a cold start, there will be insufficient flow of air to atomise this petrol – the plug ends become soaked and consequently won't spark!

Pull the main fuel line from the carburettor (it is as well to wrap a cloth around the pipe end before removing it because if the pump is working then there will be residual pressure in the system) and place the end in a jar or similar container. Have an assistant turn the engine over for a few seconds in order that the pump operates. If no fuel is forthcoming, the fuel pump could be faulty or the in-line filter blocked.

If fuel is available but the engine still won't start, then it could be flooded, which should have been apparent when you inspected the (wet, smelling strongly of petrol) spark plugs. The engine can flood because either the choke jams or too much choke has been applied for the conditions, because the carburettor float jams or more commonly the float chamber inlet needle is held in the open position by dirt. To clear dirt from the inlet valve, pinch the fuel line with the engine turning over so that the float chamber fuel level drops – then release the line and the gush of fuel through the inlet valve will normally do the trick.

FUEL. Fuel injection Beetles.

DO NOT try to test for fuel delivery, because the fuel pressure is maintained from 25 psi upwards, even when the engine is switched off and, if you were to start tinkering with the fuel lines, the fuel could spray everywhere. DON'T TOUCH IT!

If no electrical or ignition problems can be found, call in the cavalry.

ENGINE STARTS, BUT RUNS LUMPILY AND BACKFIRES WHEN REVVED

This is not a common fault, but can occur when one or more spark plugs or leads are faulty. Un-burnt fuel mixture from the affected cylinder(s) passes into the exhaust manifold, where it can be ignited by hot or still-burning gasses from other cylinders which causes it to explode, and hence the backfiring. Check each plug and lead in turn as already described for a spark — and remember — even brand new sparking plugs and leads CAN prove faulty — take nothing for granted.

ENGINE WANTS TO FIRE BUT WON'T RUN

This is normally a sign of fuel starvation, caused by a blocked fuel filter, non-functioning choke on cold mornings or air induction (air leaking into the carburettor or inlet manifold). Check the fuel delivery as already described and check for air induction through the vacuum advance pipe connections on the inlet manifold and distributor.

ENGINE TICKS OVER POORLY ON THREE CYLINDERS BUT ALL FOUR FIRE WHEN REVVED

This admittedly rare fault is normally caused by a break in a copper cored plug lead. A breakage can occur which is temporarily 'welded' as the engine revs but breaks again on tickover when engine movement is insufficient to hold the 'weld'. Disconnect each lead in turn until the faulty one is found.

Alternatively, a weakened mixture in one cylinder can lead to missing at tickover but normal firing at higher revolutions. This can be caused by a faulty or damaged inlet manifold gasket, by the vacuum advance pipe connection or — where fitted — the servo vacuum pipe. Check the pipe(s) for leakage.

UNRELIABLE STARTERS/ 'PROBLEM' CARS

Some cars seem never able to be relied upon to start first time every time. Some won't start with the engine cold; others with the engine hot. Some cars never seem to give their best and can appear un-tuneable. In either case, give the car a major service, which entails replacing most ignition components and setting up the timing and carburation correctly (the carburation is best set by professionals; all UK MOT testing stations now have exhaust gas analysers with which they can get it spot on).

Also, replace any filters in the fuel delivery system and check the fuel pump output as already described. Full overhaul kits for the fuel pump are available to restore the pump to full working condition.

If you don't feel able to do this then have the car serviced by a specialist. It is worth having the cylinder compression checked (this only takes a few minutes and won't cost too much)

An engine needs a good strong spark at the plugs during cold starts when the choke enriches the mixture. You can test the resistance readings of the primary and secondary windings with a multi-meter — if you don't have a test meter but suspect that the coil is on the way out then replace it.

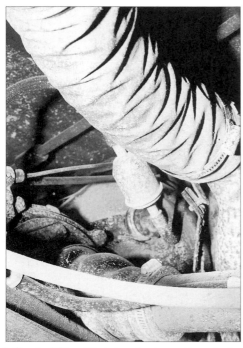

Throttle spindle – squirting on oil to check for air induction. If the tickover temporarily rises, the throttle spindle bushes are shot.

In-line fuel filter. If fuel starvation is a problem, check whether a previous owner fitted an in-line fuel filter.

or buying a meter and testing it yourself. If one or more cylinders are substantially down, then squirt a little engine oil through the spark plug hole and re-test. The oil will temporarily improve the piston ring seal and, if the compression rises with the addition of the oil, the fault is connected with the piston rings and/or worn cylinder bores (a re-bore and oversize pistons are needed) – if there is no change then the valves are the culprit and a cylinder head(s) overhaul is required.

Provided that the engine is in reasonable condition – the cylinder heads are not carbonned or cracked, the head gaskets are intact and the valves and their seats not damaged (all of which will be revealed during a de-coke) – fundamental problems with major fuel or ignition components are the most likely cause of unreliable starting, intermittent perfor-

mance/high fuel consumption, pinking and other long-term problems.

Given that the engine (which, if suspect, can be swapped for an exchange reconditioned unit) is in good condition and that no apparent faults lie in the ignition or fuel delivery systems, many long-term problems can be cured by exchanging the distributor or the carburettor for reconditioned units. Typical faults include air induction through the throttle flap spindle bushes (which, on a reconditioned carburettor, will have been reamed out and re-bushed) and wear in the distributor. A rough and ready check for air induction via the spindles is to spray a little carburettor cleaner, WD40 or even engine oil onto the spindle ends. This temporarily seals them (if they are leaking) and if the engine now runs at higher tickover revolutions then you have traced the cause of the problem.

Distributor wear can be traced by checking the dwell angle with a good automotive multimeter (the dwell angle is the percentage or angle of the distributor shaft rotation during

Measuring voltage drop across points. Anything more than one-third of a volt means that new points are needed.

If you buy a multi-meter, try to obtain one which shows dwell angle, engine revs etc.

which the points are closed, when the coil primary winding is charging) – a fluctuating dwell angle reading indicates wear in the distributor shaft bearings and results in equal variations in ignition timing. Too small a dwell angle gives a weak spark.

If you possess an automotive multi-meter then there is very little in the ignition system which you cannot test to find faults. Probably the most frequently used scale is the resistance reading (ohms) which allows you to locate disconnections (open circuits), test the coil windings and various connections. Working as a voltmeter, a multi-meter can be used to measure voltage drop across components and connections. Perhaps more importantly, it can measure voltage drop across the points when connected to the low tension lead and a good earth – anything more than 0.3V is unaccept-

able and usually indicates resistance across the points or occasionally between the base plate and the distributor body. Automotive multi-meters don't cost too much, and are well worth investing in. The author uses a Gunson Test Tune which, in addition to tracing simple open circuits (disconnections) can be used to test battery condition and charging, dwell angle, voltage drop and earth leakage. Costing less than a full professional service, such meters are highly recommended.

Air induction can be difficult to pin down because the air could – assuming all fastenings are tight – be entering via a damaged inlet manifold gasket or vacuum pipe, or the carburettor via the throttle spindle or the vacuum advance pipe. The usual symptom of air induction is lumpy tickover. Obviously, a portable exhaust gas tester will allow you to discover any such symptoms, although a spindle leak can be proven by putting a little carburettor oil on the spindle ends as already described which – if there is induction – will make the mixture richer.

INTERMITTENT FAULTS

Some problems occur only when the car is underway, perhaps at a specific speed. One such intermittent problem – engine misfiring – defied all my own attempts to track down the cause. Eventually, I took the car to the garage and had it wired up to the Cypton. According to the Crypton, the ignition system was set spot-on and there were no electrical losses; the carburation was also fine, and exhaust emission readings were well within limits. The fault simply wasn't there! It was not until the engine had been held at a steady 3,000 rpm for three or four minutes that it started missing and the Crypton showed that the HT voltage was disappearing for a second or so. The culprit had to be either the coil or the condenser – the condenser was replaced, and this cured the problem.

Intermittent faults can be real pigs to track down, simply because you cannot make them happen when you want them to! Most intermittent faults are caused by the ignition system and, in the absence of a Crypton, you can have little alternative to renewing the main ignition components, starting with the coil and condenser – which, in my case, would have cured the misfiring problem.

ON-ROAD BREAKDOWNS

The first rule of dealing with breakdowns on the road is not to panic, but to ensure that the car is parked in a safe place. In the case of a motorway this means the hard shoulder, and for safety's sake it is best to get any passengers out of the car and up the embankment. On ordinary roads as well as motorways, set out a warning triangle to advertise the presence of your car in plenty of time for following drivers, especially if you are unable to get the car fully off the road.

Once you are satisfied that everything is safe, investigate the fault. Unless the fault can be traced and rectified quickly, it is always advisable to try to summon assistance at the earliest opportunity. You can waste hours fruitlessly looking for fuel or ignition faults (the most common causes of breakdowns), only to eventually discover that a component has totally failed and that repair is impossible without replacement.

A breakdown can become an emergency if, for instance, you continue to drive whilst ignoring the signs of an electrical fire starting, or if the car should come to a halt on a narrow road in thick fog. Again, don't panic, but try to move the car to a safer position, set out a warning triangle for other road users and get any passengers out of harm's way.

'ICING' – ENGINE 'DIES' AFTER A MILE OR TWO

When air is drawn down through the carburettor throat, its pressure drops, as already stated. One side-effect of this is that its temperature also drops – to freezing. Now, if the air being drawn into the carburettor is humid, the water droplets can freeze into ice, which usually builds up inside the inlet manifold (you will usually also see ice forming on the outside of the down pipe from the carb). The build-up of ice restricts the effective internal diameter of the manifold, the engine does not receive enough fuel/air mixture and, unless the revs are kept up, the engine will die.

This phenomenon is known as 'icing' and you can obtain special heater kits which warm the inlet manifold more quickly to prevent it. I'm lucky in this respect; one mile from my home I'm on a clear road and able to keep the car rolling until the heat from the engine melts the ice and power is restored. If the engine stops altogether a mile or so into your journey, look at the down pipe and, if you see ice, don't try to start the engine straight away. Close the engine bay lid to retain what heat there is, leave it for a few minutes and heat within the engine compartment will melt the ice and the engine will re-start. Those who, a mile into their daily journey, are caught in traffic, might find that

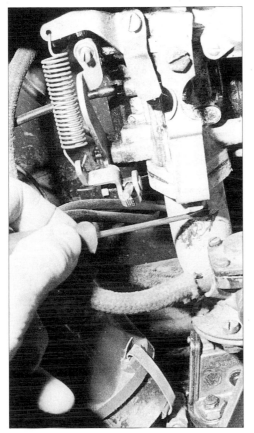

Manifold with icing. The Beetle is particularly prone to carburettor/manifold icing. The temperature of air sucked through the system drops to the point at which moisture in the air freezes. This external icing on the manifold shows just how cold it can get until the engine bay warms up. In extreme conditions, the effective internal diameter of air passages can be reduced by the build-up of ice inside the manifold. You drive a mile, and the engine refuses to tick over and dies unless you are able to keep the revs up. If the engine dies on you after a mile or two, leave it for a couple of minutes, after which the ice will have melted. If your Beetle suffers excessively from icing, check that the flap in the air filter which directs warm air into the engine is functioning correctly. Manifold heaters designed to overcome icing are available.

the engine regularly dies from icing – if so, pre-heat the engine compartment; run the engine for a couple of minutes, then leave it for a further few minutes, before starting the journey.

ENGINE 'DIES' OR LOSES POWER

The most common breakdown is when the engine dies or slowly loses power, and – terminal engine problems excepted – this will be due to a fault with either the ignition or the fuel delivery system. Before trying to trace the fault, examine the ignition wiring and the fuel system for danger signs, such as smoke from burning wire insulation or neat fuel which may have escaped from a fuel line or the carburettor. If there is a strong smell of petrol under the engine bay lid, inside the car or underneath the car then clear passengers and bystanders from the vicinity and summon professional assistance. If all appears safe, then begin to trace the fault.

If you have just driven through a heavy rain storm, puddle or ford then check first for damp which allows the charge in the high tension leads to earth itself. If the high tension leads or their caps, the distributor or any other part of the ignition system is wet then simply dry it off with a clean cloth, spray on a little water repellent oil if you carry it in the car and try to start the engine.

In dry conditions, if the engine died suddenly without any warning signs then the fault (if electrical) obviously affect all four plugs at once – look firstly for a disconnection within the ignition circuit, starting at the distributor to HT lead and moving back through the system. If the engine misfired before losing power or stopping then start by checking the spark plug caps, then move backwards through the ignition circuit. Bear in mind that ignition faults are most probably the single greatest cause of breakdowns, and check this out first.

If no ignition fault can be traced, then the problem may lie with the fuel delivery. There is a strong argument at this stage for calling in assistance, if you have not already done so. Clear any passengers from the car, and quickly check for leakage in the fuel lines.

Fuel delivery problems usually mean that either no fuel is being delivered to the carburettors or that too much fuel is being taken in by the carburettor. The former fault usually lies with the fuel pump, or a blocked filter (or most commonly an empty fuel tank!) and the latter with a sticking float. Unless you know what you are doing, call for assistance.

ENGINE LOSES POWER AND STOPS

Unless you have run out of fuel (in which case the engine would have been coughing and spluttering for a short time before it stopped) then you could have a disconnection or component failure in the ignition system (check as for engine which won't start) or, alternatively, fuel flow might be intermittent. The causes of this can be a blocked fuel tank breather (remove the filler cap and listen for a rush of air into the filler neck) a dirty fuel filter or fuel pump problems.

However, the engine could be overheating. This is a serious condition which can, if ignored, become terminal for the engine. Let the engine cool before checking the oil level – if this is low, don't run the engine unless the leakage can be traced and stemmed, and the oil topped up. If the oil level is OK then check that the thermostat is indeed opening the flaps in the fan shroud – do not run the engine unless you are sure that the problem has been rectified.

ENGINE STOPS WITHOUT WARNING

This is almost invariably caused by an ignition fault. Check this as already described.

BREAKDOWN SERVICES

Some breakdown causes cannot be fixed at the roadside, and if you are unable to quickly establish the fault then it is advisable to summon assistance at the earliest opportunity. I reported a non-starting car to one breakdown company at around 9.00 am one day when I was away from home and did not have access to the necessary tools to trace the fault myself. The breakdown service concerned relied on local garages to respond to any calls. The one-man-band they contacted in my case (a Sunday) was out playing golf, and eventually arrived at 6.00 pm – nine hours after the fault was reported!

My advice is to enrol in a service which is recommended by classic car magazines or a Beetle Owners' club because, if you are let down by such a company, then you can report the incident to the press or club and usually obtain some form of redress. Don't rely on back-street operations, but always choose a reputable, nation-wide operation.

Always opt for a service which offers special memberships for classic car owners, because many operations won't cover, for instance, cars over ten years of age. Buy the best you can.

DEVELOPING PROBLEMS

Many problems develop slowly and even those faults which have serious consequences will often only be apparent from their symptoms i.e., side-effects. For instance, a partially blocked fuel filter can make the mixture too lean and, in time, this can wreck the engine unless rectified. The symptom which will be most apparent is engine overheating. The same symptom, however, can equally signal too-advanced ignition timing, a loose fan belt, low oil level and a host of other faults.

When a symptom such as overheating becomes apparent, its cause should be traced and rectified as soon a possible.

Not every developing fault encountered on a journey will necessarily lead to a breakdown before the destination is reached, although there are several problems which can arise which should be investigated the moment it is safe to stop the car. Such faults include a sudden drop in oil pressure, an unexplained rise in

Exhaust paste. 'Popping' or backfiring on the overrun is usually caused by a holed exhaust (though check out the exhaust manifold flanges as well). When exhausts begin to rust, they reach a stage at which they are too far gone to be welded, but you can sometimes lengthen their lives by applying exhaust paste. Get all the rust off, apply the paste and run the engine up to normal operating temperature to harden the paste.

engine temperature or any apparent electrical fault, whether constant or intermittent. All of these faults can lead in a very short space of time to serious (and invariably expensive) problems. A drop in oil pressure might allow the engine to run long enough to get you to your destination, but you could wreck the engine in the process.

A rise in engine temperature is not a fault in itself but a symptom of a serious fault which could cause extensive engine damage if left unattended. An electrical fault could start an electrical fire at any time, so take these very seriously indeed. Any unusual noises warrant investigation at the earliest opportunity. In addition to engine noises such as knocking or pinking, listen for new noises from the transmission or suspension, and for suddenly excessive road/tyre noise (which may be accompanied by steering wheel vibration – which also warrants investigation).

Pinking (a harmless-sounding tinkling noise which is usually heard with the engine under load) could be caused by air induction and hence a weak mixture, by too-advanced ignition, engine overheating (non-functioning thermostat or faulty water pump) or by several other faults – the noise is made by the pistons as they tip in the bore because the mixture is being ignited too early – the long-term consequences are very expensive, so get it seen to at the earliest opportunity.

It takes experience to be able to listen to an on-road noise and pin-point the cause, and the best person to bring in if your car develops a noise which you cannot yourself identify is an experienced mechanic – he or she will have heard and will be able to identify most noises. If you try to discover the source of a noise yourself, you might never succeed, because noise can carry from its actual source and appear to emanate from a different part of the car. Call for a mechanic!

Sometimes, these warning signs lead to problems which can be dealt with there and then, sometimes, it is up to the driver to decide whether to carry on and risk damage to the car or whether to summon assistance.

Of the faults which can be dealt with, if the engine is pinking, look firstly for an induction air leak. If an irregular knocking noise can be heard, check the tightness of exhaust, suspension and other fittings. If tyre noise can be heard or if vibration is suddenly felt through the steering wheel, check the tyres for bulges or other damage, and then fit the spare to the appropriate corner.

SURVIVING ROADWORKS AND QUEUES

Why are roadworks always accompanied by signs which state that such and such an authority apologises for any delay caused when we all know perfectly well that roadworks are sited and timed to cause maximum delays to the greatest number of drivers? To make matters worse, and on a personal note, they always choose the hottest days of the year to resurface roads on which I want to drive – risking an overheated engine in the slow moving queue of traffic caused by said resurfacing. I strongly suspect a conspiracy.

Serious overheating demands that the engine is stopped. This can cause a temporary traffic jam, but the alternative is to let the engine seize and cause a more permanent jam. Pull off the road anywhere safe, turn off the engine and raise the engine bay lid to speed cooling. Call for assistance.

The worst place to have an overheating engine is in a queue on a motorway when the hard shoulder has been pressed into service as an extra lane. There is simply nowhere to go, and you have the choice of risking a real breakdown or causing a temporary traffic jam by switching off the ignition.

Always ensure that the oil level is OK and that the generator drive belt is in excellent condition and correctly tensioned before setting out on a long journey.

TROUBLE SHOOTING

The following notes omit one potential cause of every one of the problems listed – major mechanical failure. Remember – if a fault cannot be traced quickly, it is best to summon assistance rather than waste time looking for a problem which you might not be able to deal with at the roadside.

ENGINE REFUSES TO START FROM COLD/ENGINE WON'T TURN OVER

Loose/corroded battery connections
Engine earth strap fixings loose
Battery flat – low electrolyte level
Starter connections loose
Solenoid faulty/loose connections
Starter jammed

ENGINE TURNS OVER BUT WON'T FIRE

Don't pump the throttle!!
Fuel tank empty
Fuel pump faulty
Vapour lock in fuel system
HT lead connections poor
Coil connections poor
HT leads/distributor cap wet
HT leads faulty
Distributor cap cracked/arcing
Contact breaker points dirty/seized/gap
  incorrect
Spark plug end fittings loose
Spark plugs damaged/carbonned/oiled/wet
Spark plugs faulty/gap incorrect
Fuel pump defective/filter blocked
Engine flooded
Choke jammed on
Dirt in fuel bowl jet
Carburettor float seized

START MOTOR SPINS BUT DOES NOT TURN ENGINE

Starter motor bolts loose
Pinion sticking

ENGINE STARTS, BUT RUNS LUMPILY AND BACKFIRES WHEN REVVED

Spark plug/HT lead faulty

ENGINE WANTS TO FIRE
BUT WON'T RUN

Blocked air filter
Non-functioning choke
Air induction via vacuum pipe on inlet
manifold

ENGINE TICKS OVER POORLY ON THREE
CYLINDERS BUT ALL FOUR FIRE WHEN
REVVED

Breakage in copper-cored HT lead

ON-ROAD BREAKDOWNS
ENGINE MISFIRES OR LOSES POWER

Fuel tank empty
Fuel filler cap breather blocked
Ignition components wet
Ignition open circuit
Faulty fuel pump
Blocked fuel filter
Sticking carburettor float

ENGINE LOSES POWER AND STOPS

Blocked fuel tank cap breather
Blocked fuel filter
Faulty fuel pump
Engine overheating

ENGINE STOPS WITHOUT WARNING

Ignition component failure

DEVELOPING PROBLEMS
ENGINE OVERHEATS

Broken/slack generator drive belt
Thermostat faulty
Engine oil level low
Brakes binding
Weak fuel mixture
Ignition timing fault

ENGINE BACKFIRES ON OVERRUN

Exhaust system leakage/burnt exhaust valve(s)
Leakage from heat exchangers/exhaust

'GET-YOU-HOME' TIPS

The following comprises advised courses of action which may enable you to effect temporary repairs; the advice must be used only in cases where it does not contravene prevailing national or local laws, and the author and publisher can assume no responsibility if advice does conflict with prevailing law.

In the UK, it is an offence to drive an 'unsafe' car on the public highway and, in fact, some Police Officers are being specially trained to detect any of 200 possible faults which render a car unsafe – they are empowered to prohibit the use of the car there and then. Serious problems which make a car unsafe to drive – including brake failure, lighting failure, almost any electrical, suspension or hydraulic problem – MUST be rectified before the car is driven.

Many developing faults give 'early warning' symptoms which the experienced driver can often recognise, which gives you the opportunity to head straight for the nearest repair workshop or to stop the car before the fault develops further.

DEALING WITH ON-ROAD FAULTS

Broken generator drive belt. The generator drive belt is driven by the crankshaft pulley and drives the engine cooling fan and dynamo on early cars, alternator on later cars. The usual first symptom of the broken belt is that the ignition light illuminates, signifying that the battery is no longer being charged.

A car with a broken belt can be driven gently for a very short distance (a hundred yards? – after that, you're risking it) but the lack of cooling effect from the fan will quickly overheat the engine, and can result in internal engine damage. A battery in good condition will be able to power the ignition circuit for some time, although use of the lights, wiper motor, heater fan and especially the starter motor will reduce this greatly.

It is best to drive the car only to a known (very) nearby place of safety – don't drive away in the hope of finding something – the engine could seize and leave you stranded in an even worse place.

Temporary fan belts are available, although those setting out on a long journey would do better to pack a spare belt, plus a 21mm spanner and screwdriver with which to fit it. The traditional 'get-you-home' ploy involves using a nylon stocking to make a temporary belt; variations include using leather belts and rope; the author has thankfully not had to resort to such botch-ups – pack a spare drive belt!

Broken Throttle Cable. Set the tickover to 1,500 rpm or slightly more, then change up through the gears to reach a top speed of circa 30 mph – and hope that you don't have to climb any steep hills! Do this only in order to reach a nearby place of safety or repair – don't try to cover any real distance or ever use this ploy on major roads!

Blowing Exhaust. Most of the sealing materials which the author has used offer strictly temporary repair – to make gums or bandage repair kits longer-lasting cover them with thin steel (from a drinks can, which can be cut with scissors) fastened with jubilee clips.

Binding Brakes. Allow to cool. The problem could be hydraulic or mechanical – unless you can find the reason for the binding and rectify it, progress should be limited to very short hops, stopping frequently and for long periods to allow the brakes to cool fully. Best to summon a recovery service.

Shattered Windscreen. Place cloth on scuttle and bonnet to catch glass, then use heavily gloved hand or implement to push ALL shattered glass out. Open windows and quarterlights to allow air to pass through cab.

DON'T

Hot wire the ignition – you'll have no indicators for one thing, and few of today's drivers recognise hand signals.

Drive with a flat tyre – it will soon come off the rim and damage both tyre and wheel – perhaps beyond repair.

Tolerate intermittent trifling electrical faults – some can suddenly become serious, permanent and even terminal (both for the car and occupants).

Drive with seized brakes – fire hazard.

Live with any 'temporary' repair for a second longer than absolutely necessary.

Drive with an engine which is overheating.

Replace a blown fuse with anything other than a fuse of the same rating – if this, too, blows, it is a warning of a short to earth which could directly cause an in-car fire.

NEVER

Drive with tyres under or over-inflated. This jeopardises roadholding, compromises handling and gives high tyre wear.

Use unleaded fuel unless the cylinder heads have been specially modified.

TERMINAL FAULTS (SEND FOR THE CAVALRY)

These faults – thankfully – are all very rare, and most drivers will never suffer any of them. Should you be one of the unfortunate few, don't waste time – summon assistance at the earliest opportunity!

MECHANICAL SEIZURE Engine – Transaxle. Engine. Allow to cool fully. Don't use starter, but place in fourth gear and try to rock car backwards and forwards to see whether seizure has freed. Unless cause can be established and rectified (unlikely), don't run engine.

Transaxle. Forget it! Call for assistance.

Fuel Pump Failure. Unless another pump can be fitted, summon assistance.

Forecourt and Service Data

Fuel
4-Star Leaded   9.2 Gallons

Engine oil
Multigrade SAE 20W 50   4.4 pints (2.5 litres)

Transaxle oil
EP gear oil SAF 80   4.4 pints (2.5 litres)

Tyre pressures

5.60-15PR Crossply	16 psi	front
	24 psi	rear
	26 psi	loaded rear
155 SR15 Radial	18 psi	front
	27psi	rear

Spare tyre/washer bottle pressure   40 psi

Tightening torques

	psi	kg m
Oil sump drain plug	25	3.5
Oil strainer plate	5	0.7
Generator pulley	43	6.0
Transaxle oil filler and drain plugs	14	2.0

Spark Plugs
Gap   .23"   0.6mm

Generator drive belt deflection
.5" max.

Ignition timing markings
One crank pulley notch; the correct timing mark for all Beetles EXCEPTING 1300s made after October 1971, on which the mark signifies 0 degrees (TDC).

Two marks, use L/H mark (7.5 degrees - R/H shows 10 degrees) EXCEPT 1200s with an engine serial number between 5000000 and 9725086, timed 10 degrees BTDC (use the R/H mark).

Three marks; 1600 B series engines are 0 degrees (L/H mark)

1500s; 7.5 degrees (centre mark) excepting H series between 087928 and 1124670, timed 0 degrees (L/H mark).

1200; 0, 7.5 and 10 degrees, with 0 far left; D series between 0675000 and 1268062 are 0 degrees, engines between 5000000 and 9725086 are 10 degrees.

Confusing? your bet! If in doubt, consult a workshop manual for the specific year and model concerned, or take the car to a service centre with Crypton or Sun equipment, and ask them to make the appropriate timing mark for you.

Index

Page references in *italic* refer to captions.

A posts *19*, 25, 81
abrasives 91-2
accumulators 120
aerosol paints *103*
air ducts 31
air filters *52*, 56
air induction 133
air/fuel mix 119, 123, 130
alternators 120, 121
ammeters 67
annual servicing 51, *52-3*, 53
antifreeze 6
Apollo HULPs 92-3, *93*
arcing 130
atmospheric pollution 119-20
automatic chokes 11, 119
automotive multi-meters 133
axle stands *28*, 29, 36, 39
axles 11, *11*, 44-5, *44-5*, *107*

B posts 25, 81
backfiring 131, *137*
Ball, Terry 42
barrier paints 90
batteries 28, 29, 35, *35*, 66, 78, *79*, 120, 121, 125-6
battery chargers *127*
battery connections 125-6, *125*
Beach Buggies *21*
Beetle 1100 series 10-11
Beetle 1200 series 11, 48
Beetle 1300 series 11, *11*, 48
Beetle 1500 series 11
Beetle Specialist Workshop 42, *102*
Beetle Type 60, 8
Beetle variant 11-12
binding brakes 69, 140
bleeding braking systems *52*
blocked fuel systems 136
blown exhausts 140
body fillers *see* fillers
body rot 7, 12-14, *12-13*, *18-19*, 20
body shells 81-2, *82*

body work 13-14, *18-19*, 59, 82-3, 88-92, *89-90*
body work restoration 71, 82-4
bonnets 6
bottle jacks 29, *29*
boxer motors *117*, 123
brake adjusters 36-7, *38*
brake drums 37-8, *36-7*, *52*
brake fluid 28, 29, *34* 99
brake hoses 36
brake pads 38-9, *38*
brake shoes 35-8, *36-8*
brake wheel cylinders *53*
braking systems 10-11, 35-8, *36-8*, 44, *52*, 56, 69, *102*, 140
breakdown services 136
breakdowns 7, 116-40, *116-40*
bump starting 126
bumpers *13,111*
butt welding 84
butterfly flaps 119
buying a car 7, 12-17, 20-1

cable brakes 11
car prices 20, *24*
car radios 67-9, *68*
carbon monoxide (C0) 119
carburettors 116, 118, 120, 123, 132
carpets 64-5
catalytic converters 70
cellulose paints 92, 98
chassis 13, *13*, 81-2
off-road *22*
checklists 138-9
choice of car 20-3, 25
choke controls 6, 69
chokes 6, 11, *118*, 119, 125
clutch assemblies *100*, *102*
clutch release bearing 101
coil windings 122
cold starting 130
compressors 92
condensers 40, *40*, 123, *129*
conductors 121
contact breaker points 46
coolant temperature gauges 67
cooling systems 29, 31-2, *32*, 39

crankshafts 45, 46, 48, 49-50
crash damage *16*
crimping tools *66*, *109*
Crypton timing equipment 48, 134
custom cars 31-2, *23*, 60, *61*, 62, *63*, 64-9, *65-6*, 68
cylinder compression 131-2
cylinders 118, 123

damp 135
dashboards 67
demisting systems 62
dents 90, 91, *93*
Dinitrol 103
dipsticks *29*, 30
disc brakes 11, 38-9, *38*, *52*
disposal:
of engine oil 42, 44
distilled water 29, 35
distributor caps 40, *40*, 123
distributors 122-3, 133-4
door seals *81*, *89*
door trims *110*
doors 53, 81, *81*, *89*
drive shafts 11, *44*
driver comfort 59-60, *60-1*, 62, *63*, 64
driving techniques 70
drying times 98, 100
dynamic timing 49-50, *49*
dynamos 120, 121

earths 121-2
electric nibblers *63*, 64
electrical faults 106, 140
electrical fires 122
electrical systems 28, 31, 35, 54, *112-13*, 120-4
electricity 120-1
electrolytes 121
Electronic Control Units (ECU's) 120
electronic fuel injection 120
engine bays *96*, *103*, *107*, *113*
engine capacity 11
engine oil 29-31, *29-31*
engine oil change 42-4, *43*
engine oil disposal 42, 44

engine seizure 140
engines *15*, *117*, 123-4
estimates 114-15
etch primers 98
exhaust systems 32, 39, 123, 133, 140
exhaust valves 123
expert advice 14-17, *23*
export markets 10

fan belts 140
fault-finding 7, 116, 124-6, *127-9*, 128-39, *131-3*, *135*, *137*
feeler gauges 46, *47*
filler flatting 91
fillers 13, 91-2
fires 122
flat tyres 124-5, *124-5*, 140
flitch panels 19
floorpans 87
foot pumps 29, *33*
forecourt data 141
front suspension *16*
fuel 28, 70, 118-19, 123-4, 140
fuel atomisation 120
fuel consumption 10, 69 70
fuel filters 119, 132
fuel injection 27, 28, 50, 119-20, 130
fuel pump failures 140
fuel systems *102*, 116, 118-20, *118*, *130*, 136
fuses *112*, 122, 140

gearboxes 11
generator drive belts 31, *31*, 41-2, *41*, 139-40
grounds *see* earths
guarantees 20-1
Gunson's Gas testers 56
Gunson Test Tunes 133, *133*
hand brakes 37, 56
headlight alignment 55-6
heat generation 120-1
heating systems *12*, 13, *18*, *19*, 62, *87-8*

High Tension (HT) leads 122, 123, 128, *129*, 130
High Volume, Low Pressure (HVLP) spray outfits 92-3, *93*
historical survey 6-7, 8, *9*, 10-12
Hitler, Adolf 8
HPI Autodata 17

hub caps *124*
hydraulic brakes 10-11
hydraulic fluid 29, 33, *34*, 35
hydrocarbons 119
Hypoid SAE 90 oil 45

icing 134-5, *135*
idling speed 51, *51*
ignition advance 124
ignition systems 121, 122-3, 124, 125 6, *125*, *127-8*, 135, 140
ignition timing 46, *47*, 48-50, *48-9*
illegal sales 7, 17
indicators *109*
in-car entertainment (ICE) 67-9, *68*
inspection procedures 40-1
instruments 67
insulators 123
interior paint work *89*
interior trim 64-5, *65*, 81
intermittent faults 134, 140

jacks 27-8, *27*, *28*, 29, 36 7, 39

Karmann convertibles 11
keying *see* surface keying
leakage's 31
lighting systems 35, 54, 55-6, 66
luggage bays 6, *6*, 33, *34*, 35, *107*
MacPherson struts 11, *11*, *19*, *25*, 81
magnetic fields 120-1
maintenance *see* servicing
masking-up *94*
MGA series 10
Mig welding 75, *76*, *83*, 84, 86-8
Minis 10
mixture setting 50-1, *50-1*
mobile welders 88
monthly servicing 35-9, *35-8*
Morris Minors 10
MOT failure points *35*, *44*, 53-6
MOT tests 14, 16, 20, *36*, *44*, 51, 53-6, 83-4, 106

Newton, Bill *61*
noises:
    reasons for 137
NSU 12

off-road chassis *22*
oil *see* engine oil
oil burning 31

oil loss 31, *45*
oil pressure 136-7
oil pressure gauges 67
oil seals *37*
oil strainers 42, *43*
older cars 7
on-road breakdowns 134-40, *135*, *137*
overcoating 90
overheating 138, 140
owners clubs 10, 14, 136
oxides of nitrogen (NOX) 119

paint contamination 92
paint flatting *89*, 90, *93*, *96-7*, 98, 100
paint reaction *95*
paint spraying *see* spraying
paints 59, *59*, 98
paint work 88-91, *89-90*, 98, 99-100, *100*
performance 11, 119
petrol *see* fuel
photographic records 22-3, 78, *79*, 115
pinking 137
piston strokes 123
pistons 123
plug welding *86*
point gaps 40, *40*, 122, *133*
pollution *see* atmospheric pollution
poor workmanship 108-9
Porsche, Ferdinand 8
power loss 135-6
primary windings 122-3
primers 92, *94*, *96-7*, 98
    see also paints
pro-am restoration 115
problem cars 131-4
production models 10-12
production modifications 78, *79*
professional advice *see* expert advice
professional restoration 22-3, 71, 106, 108-9, 112-15
professional servicing 56-7
professional welders 88
punctures *see* flat tyres

rain gutters *97*
rear brakes *38*
rebuilding 100, *101-14*, 106, 108-9, 112-15
reconstruction 77

see also restoration
regulators see accumulators
reliability 116
  see also breakdowns
renovation 77
  see also restoration
repair panels 84
resistors 120-1
restoration 7, 14, 18, 20, 22, 24-6, 25, 71-115, 71-115
restoration workshops 112-13
road works 138
rocker boxes 45
rotor arms 123
Royal Electrical and Mechanical Engineers (REME) 8

safety precautions 27-8,27-8, 42, 45, 73, 75, 98, 112, 122, 134
sanders 91
scissors jacks 29
scratches 101
seat belts 53
seam welding 86
seats 53, 64, 65
secondary windings 122
service data 141
servicing 7, 20,26-66, 26-66,
  annual 51, 52-3, 53
  longer term 53
  monthly 35-9, 35-8
  professional 56-7
  six monthly 39-46, 39-51, 48-51
  under car 31, 58-9
  weekly 29-33, 29-35, 35
shattered windscreens 140
shorting out 121-2, 126
silencers 123
six monthly servicing 39-46, 39-51, 48-51
slave labour 8
socket sets 39
South America 11
spanner sets 39
spare parts 16
spark plugs 40, 40, 118, 122, 123, 129, 130, 131
speed see performance
split windscreens 10
spray guns 92
spraying 92, 93-7, 96-7
starter motors 28, 127
starter problems 125-6, 127-9, 128, 130-3, 131-3

starter solenoids 126, 127
starting 116, 119
static timing 48-9, 49, 50
steering boxes 42, 54
steering racks 55, 55
steering wheels 42, 54
stepped edge repairs 85-6
stolen cars see illegal sales
stone chip paints 59, 59
stripping down 78, 79-82, 81-2
stroboscope lights 39, 49
Sun timing equipment 48
sunroof fitting 62, 63, 64
surface keying 91, 98
suspension 11, 11, 54
  front 16
synchromesh gearboxes 11

tachometers 67
Tatra 8
test devices 133, 133
test runs 50
thermostats 31-2, 32, 39
thinners 98
throttle cables 140
throttle spindles 132, 133
timing marks 45-6, 47, 48
tool kits 26, 27, 39, 76-7
torsion bars 11, 16, 19, 44
tracking 32
transaxles 44-5, 44-5, 140
trolley jacks 29
troubleshooting 138-9
tyre noise 137
tyre pressures 6, 29, 32-3, 32-3, 69-70, 140
tyre tread 32-3, 54
tyres 32-3, 32-3, 36, 124-5, 124-5, 140
  see also wheels

UK car industry 10
UK market 10
under car servicing 31, 32, 58-9, 109
undercoats 98, 100
underseal 74
unleaded fuel 123-4, 140
unreliable cars see problem cars
US market 10

valve clearances 45-6, 46
valves 123
vehicle regulations 12

ventilation systems 62, 63,64
visual checks 31, 32
Volkswagen 8, 10, 11
Volkswagen Golf 12
Volkswagen K70 series 12
Volkswagen Passat 12
voltage drop 133
voltmeters 67

warning signs:
  of car problems 136-7
washing cars 57-9, 58
waxing body work 59
weekly servicing 29-33, 29-35, 35
welding 75, 76, 77-8, 83-4, 83, 85-8, 86-8
wet and dry 91-2, 93, 96, 98, 100
wheel cambers 32-3
wheel changes 29, 32, 124-5, 124-5
wheel chocks 27
wheel braces 125
wheels 33, 35, 36, 54-5, 55
  see also tyres
window winders 110
windows 80, 81, 90
windscreen washers 34, 35, 53-4, 65-6, 66
windscreen wipers 54
windscreens 10, 53, 103-6, 140
wing sections 95, 108
wiring 121, 122
  see also electrical systems
workshop manuals 27, 78
workshops 75-6